In the Company of
Seahorses

Steve Trewhella and Julie Hatcher

WILD NATURE PRESS

Published in 2017 by
Wild Nature Press
Winson House, Church Road
Plympton St. Maurice, Plymouth PL7 1NH

A CIP catalogue record for this book is available from the British Library.

ISBN 978-0-9955673-2-0

Designed by Julie Dando
Printed and bound in Slovenia on behalf of Latitude Press

10 9 8 7 6 5 4 3 2 1

www.wildnaturepress.com

Contents

Foreword

I remember talking to Steve and Julie before diving in Studland. A stiff breeze had been blowing from the south-west for a couple of days, and although it had eased so that the white horses were now galloping further down the coast, there was still a residual swell rolling in. To be honest it didn't look too promising, but their eagerness to show me 'their' bay was undimmed. Pulling on my fins, I followed Steve into the water. We swam around just above the eelgrass fronds, everything a fuzzy yellow from the stirred up sand.

An hour later I'd had enough, but Steve was still furtling in the weed, gently wafting the fronds with the palm of his hand, parting them so he could see down to the seabed. He was looking for the horses, willing them out of the murk so I might catch a glimpse too. No, we didn't find any that day, but the dive gave me an insight into just how much this place meant to him and Julie. Here were two divers with passion, enthusiasm and commitment.

Those same three words came to my mind as I read the lovely little intimate pieces of marine beastie behaviour that Steve and Julie describe in this book. You'd never witness those moments unless, like them, you'd spent many hours in the water, swimming, waiting, chilling, watching, clicking. The images they have captured only come from a tenacity that borders on obsession. The respect that they both feel for marine life, and bays of eelgrass in particular, shines through on every page.

This book deserves to be shared by all who value what's special about the seas around the UK, particularly as areas of seagrass and their diverse populations are under threat. There's little protection from too many anchors lobbed randomly off too many leisure boats. Scallop dredging is still permitted in some places, and onshore development brings subsequent run-off issues along with other forms of pollution.

It would be criminal if this book became an epitaph to seagrass meadows and seahorses rather than an inspiration that contributes to their future protection.

Doug Allan
Wildlife and documentary cameraman

The start of a love affair

Some experiences are etched so clearly in your memory, it's as if they happened yesterday.
There is one such memory that we both share.

It was the end of an enjoyable but otherwise uneventful dive in Studland Bay. We had spent an hour or so exploring the seagrass beds and, running low on air, we were heading back towards the beach. As the swaying stems were replaced by white sand, shimmering with the rippling light from above, we were stopped in our tracks by a sight straight out of a fairy tale. There, as large as life, was a beautiful, yellow seahorse with its characteristic tail curled around a seaweed frond. We could not believe our eyes and had to surface to compose ourselves and decide what to do.

In 2004 underwater digital cameras were not widely available and our 35mm Nikonos had run out of film. Understanding the importance of this rare sighting, there was no way we were leaving without a photograph. We decided that as one of us took the long walk back to the car to change the film, the other would stay with the seahorse.

Although we have seen many since, this pregnant male Spiny Seahorse holds a very special place in our hearts. He seemed so vulnerable, just metres from a busy beach with numerous boats anchored all around and passing overhead. Having spent a few minutes in his company, we watched as he slowly swam away and vanished back into the seagrass.

The significance of this seahorse goes beyond our first encounter and the ignition of our love affair with these enchanting animals. It turned out to be the first confirmed sighting of a pregnant seahorse in the United Kingdom. As such, it changed people's perception of UK seahorses overnight. Rather than just being occasional visitors, it proved they were living and breeding here and part of our national fauna.

Our first encounter, a pregnant male Spiny Seahorse, photographed on 35mm film. We had just 36 chances to get the exposure and lighting right, followed by a long, nerve-wracking few days while the film was processed before we knew if it had been successful.

INTRODUCTION

Seahorses are one of those rare creatures that are somewhere between myth and reality. They seem to break all the rules of what an animal should look like: a fish with the head of a horse, the tail of a monkey and a suit of armour encasing its body. The scientific name for seahorse is *Hippocampus* from the Greek words '*Hippo*' meaning horse and '*campus*' meaning sea monster, in recognition of its mixed-up characteristics.

The seahorse is a unique and iconic symbol of the sea and has been a source of curiosity and wonder through the ages. Everyone knows what a seahorse looks like. It is one of the most recognisable of animals, one that children learn from their earliest days. Despite this, we know very little about them, their habits and behaviours. As divers, we are in the privileged position of being able to observe seahorses and their behaviour in British waters and have done so over many years. This book documents our experiences and we hope it will inspire people to appreciate seahorses as much as we do; to understand their vulnerabilities, their needs and their place in the marine ecosystem.

Seahorses do not live in isolation but are components of a larger ecosystem. They live within a community of wildlife, with predators, prey and even close relatives. The tiny fry drift for a time as plankton before settling on the seabed. Their habitats can be sensitive and vulnerable to human activity, especially those in shallow, coastal waters. In the latter half of the book we describe the other animals that accompany seahorses along the way and the threats they all face.

Looking more horse than fish, it is easy to understand why seahorses fuelled the myths and stories of ancient civilisations.

Hippocamps were animals in ancient mythology that were half horse and half serpentine fish. They were believed to be the adult form of seahorses.

The global picture

No one is certain of the total number of seahorse species around the world. At the time of writing it is estimated that there are 48, although this number may increase as research advances our understanding. For example, studies are being carried out on the Spiny Seahorse to discover if the population found in Britain is genetically different from those in the Mediterranean and West Africa. The cryptic nature of seahorses makes them difficult to study in the wild but nevertheless, it is perhaps surprising that very few scientific studies are being carried out to learn more about them. The IUCN Red List contains 41 species of seahorse, of which it lists eleven as Vulnerable and one as Endangered. So little is known about populations of the other species that it is not possible to assess their conservation status.

An Australian Big-bellied Seahorse, *Hippocampus abdominalis*, at up to 30cm long, is one of the largest seahorse species in the world.

Seahorses have been found roughly from 50 degrees north to 50 degrees south, with most species occurring in the West Atlantic and the Indo-Pacific region.

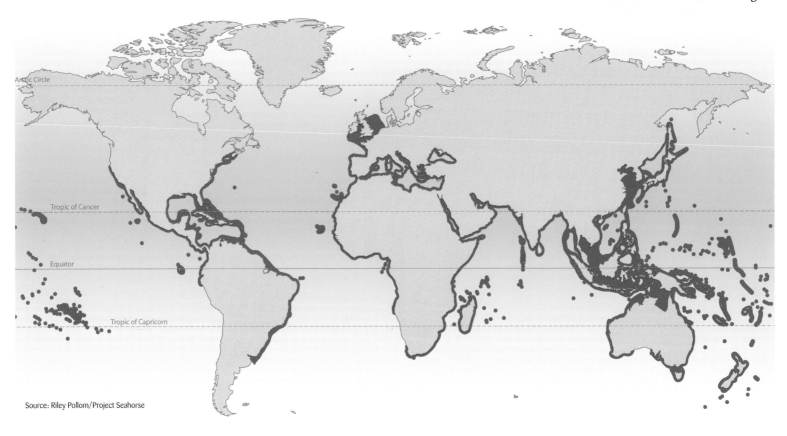

Arctic Circle

Tropic of Cancer

Equator

Tropic of Capricorn

Source: Riley Pollom/Project Seahorse

A fossilised seahorse reveals that these fish were alive in our seas between 3 and 5 million years ago during the Pliocene epoch.

Worldwide, seahorses vary in size from a tiny pygmy seahorse measuring just 2cm from the tip of its tail to the top of its head, to the large Australian Big-bellied Seahorse at up to 30cm (see page 11). Research has found that their size generally increases towards higher latitudes.

At a global scale seahorses inhabit a variety of ecosystems such as coral reefs, mangroves, and seagrass meadows in tropical and temperate waters. They are not found in the polar regions. Seahorses are an essential component of the ecosystems they inhabit, playing an important role as a predator and keeping populations of their prey in balance. They also serve as flagship species, highlighting the importance of these ecosystems and acting as an indicator of their overall health.

It is difficult to study the longevity of seahorses in the wild, and most estimates are based on studies of captive animals. Larger species tend to live longer than smaller species, with an estimated average lifespan of between 1 and 5 years. The eggs and larvae of seahorses as a group are generally larger than those of other bony fish that provide parental care, and while the number of fry produced tends to be smaller, they are more developed when born, giving them a greater chance of survival. The energy the male seahorse puts into incubating the developing young in his pouch therefore pays off, as seahorse fry are better able to cope with the harsh realities of life in the sea.

This is a rare image of a fossilised seahorse. It is an adult of the species *Hippocampus sarmaticus*, found in the Tunjice Hills in Slovenia, and measures approximately 5cm in length.

A tiny pygmy seahorse, Bargibant's Pygmy Seahorse *Hippocampus bargibanti*, camouflaged perfectly against the gorgonian coral among which it lives.

SEAHORSES OF THE BRITISH ISLES

Two species of seahorse are native to the seas around the British Isles, the Short-snouted Seahorse, *Hippocampus hippocampus* and the Spiny or Long-snouted Seahorse, *Hippocampus guttulatus*. They are members of the Sygnathidae family of fish along with seadragons and pipefish. Sygnathidae comes from the Greek meaning 'fused jaws' and refers to the snout which is common to all members of this family (see page 28).

Many people assume that seahorses are restricted to clear, tropical waters and are often surprised to learn that they are native to the colder seas around the British Isles. In fact, the rich and diverse undersea habitats around Britain are perfect for these fish, providing an abundance of their minute prey and providing the shelter they require to thrive.

Most of the records of seahorses around the British Isles are from casual sightings, many from fishermen who occasionally bring them up with fishing gear. Their cryptic nature has made it difficult to find them, let alone study them in the field. Our unique experiences in the company of seahorses in our native waters have enabled us to learn new aspects of their behaviour, their life cycle and the threats they face.

Most records of British species such as this male Spiny Seahorse come from fisherman who have found them entwined in fishing gear, or from chance encounters.

Spiny Seahorse
Hippocampus guttulatus

Size 16cm

The Spiny or Long-snouted Seahorse is a native of the British Isles. Its favoured habitat is seagrass meadows, although it is not exclusive to these and may also be found amongst seaweed. The 'spines' that give it its English name are fleshy and very variable. They may be long and branched, or short and sparse, in effect giving each individual a unique profile. Those living among seagrass tend to be shades of yellow, brown and olive green to blend in with the surrounding vegetation, while those living among algae can exhibit more variable colour.

A male Spiny Seahorse in classic pose, head held proudly, displaying his elaborate mane of fleshy 'spines'.

A Spiny Seahorse exhibiting typical evasive behaviour to avoid eye contact and hide its silhouette.

Short-snouted Seahorse
Hippocampus hippocampus

Size 16cm

The Short-snouted Seahorse is native to the seas around the British Isles. Sometimes found with the Spiny Seahorse, it generally lives in a wider range of habitats, including seagrass meadows, estuaries and other shallow coastal seabeds. Colour varies depending on the colour of its surroundings, pinky-brown being one of the commoner colours we have observed. Its body appears clean in outline as it lacks the fleshy spines of some species. It has a well-defined coronet on the top of its head and a relatively short snout compared with the Spiny Seahorse.

A classic side-on view of a Short-snouted Seahorse showing its prominent coronet and smooth outline lacking the fleshy spines of its relative.

The only pregnant male Short-snouted Seahorse we have seen. The elusive nature of this highly camouflaged creature makes it difficult to study, despite its broader choice of habitats.

ANATOMY

Seahorses, unlike most other fish, have evolved an upright posture. Although they retain most of the usual anatomical features of bony fish there are some differences that have evolved in order to fit them to their specialised lifestyle.

These diagrams show the seahorse's main physical characteristics, the visible differences between the two British species and the difference between sexes.

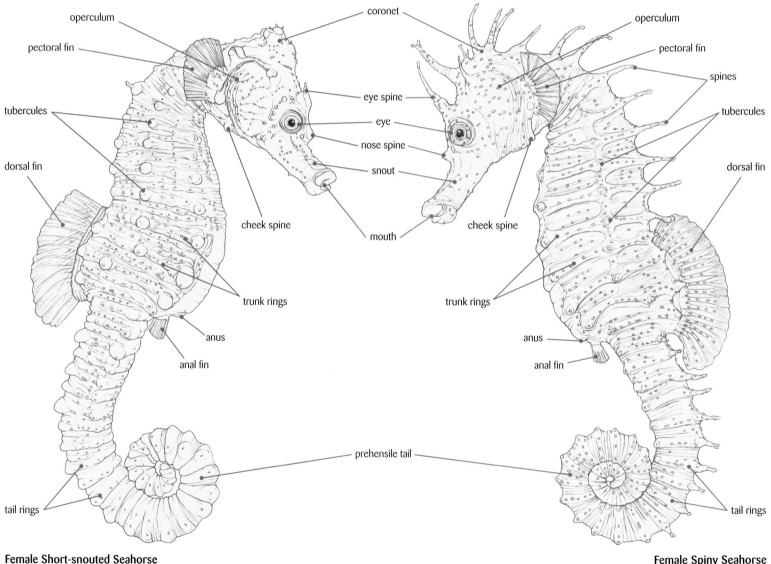

operculum · pectoral fin · tubercules · dorsal fin · coronet · eye spine · eye · nose spine · snout · cheek spine · mouth · trunk rings · anus · anal fin · prehensile tail · tail rings · operculum · pectoral fin · spines · tubercules · dorsal fin · cheek spine · trunk rings · anus · anal fin · tail rings

Female Short-snouted Seahorse

Female Spiny Seahorse

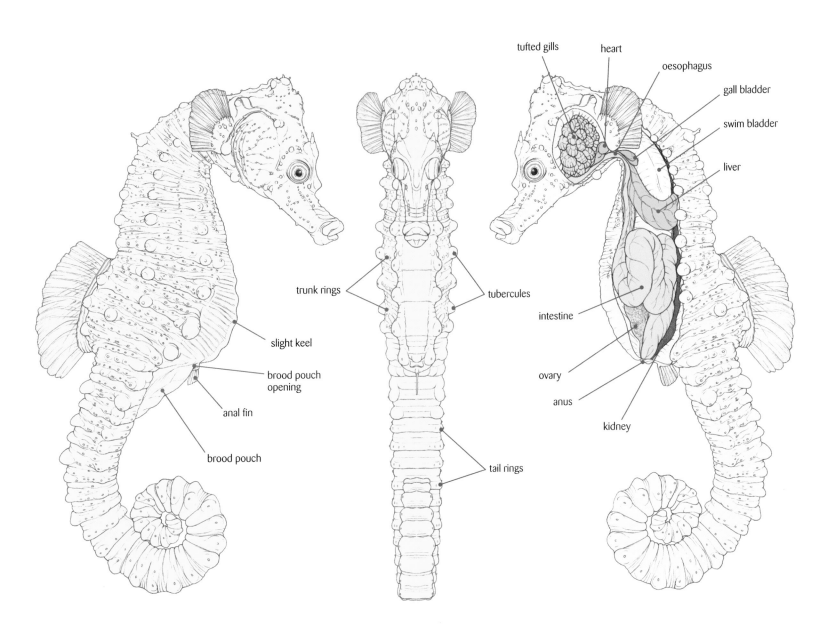

tufted gills

heart

oesophagus

gall bladder

swim bladder

liver

trunk rings

tubercules

slight keel

brood pouch
opening

anal fin

intestine

brood pouch

ovary

anus

tail rings

kidney

Male Short-snouted Seahorse

**Female Short-snouted Seahorse
front view**

**Female Short-snouted Seahorse
internal organs**

Sound and vision

Seahorses have chameleon-like eyes that move independently. While one is looking forward the other can be looking backward, giving the animal the maximum field of vision. This is useful for a fish that needs a constant supply of live food and is not capable of rapid movement or pursuit of prey. So whilst homing in on one item of prey it could already have located the next.

A number of fish species are known to communicate through sound, and some seahorses do this. They can produce clicking sounds when feeding, during courtship and when males compete over a female. The sounds are made by contact between bony structures in the head and neck.

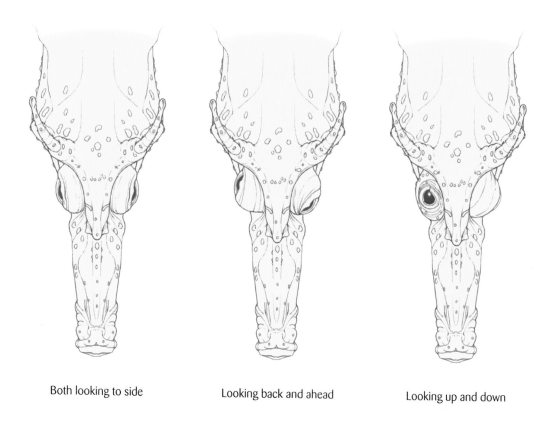

Both looking to side   Looking back and ahead   Looking up and down

Similarities between the development of seahorse and human eyes are helping scientists better understand how detailed vision develops and may lead to the ability to restore sight for people with impaired vision.

A prehensile tail

Seahorses are exceptional among fish for having a flexible tail that grips objects to anchor themselves in position. There is no tail fin, as the tail is not used for swimming. Instead it is used to stabilise and secure the animal and will wrap around any stable object including seagrass stems, seaweed or man-made items such as rope and shellfish pots. Seahorses are poor swimmers, and anchoring themselves in this way is useful when hiding from predators while providing security in strong currents and sea swell. When feeding, it gives them the flexibility to home in on their tiny prey while remaining in position. As these animals move around the seabed, the tail often appears to move independently, feeling for a suitable anchorage to wrap around, rather like an elephant's trunk sniffing out a bag of peanuts.

A perfect illustration of the way a seahorse uses its tail to grip a stable anchor while scanning for prey.

The tall Peacock Worm tube makes a good anchorage to hold onto.

A bony cage

Rather than scales, seahorses have skin stretched over a bony skeleton akin to a cage. This structure is reminiscent of an old-fashioned aeroplane made of a rigid frame with canvas stretched across it. The bones form rings around the body and also run lengthways, and where they cross they form raised bumps, sometimes with spines. This structure can clearly be seen beneath the skin and means the animal retains its extraordinary shape in death. This type of skeleton provides protection for the internal organs and also makes the fish fairly unpalatable for potential predators.

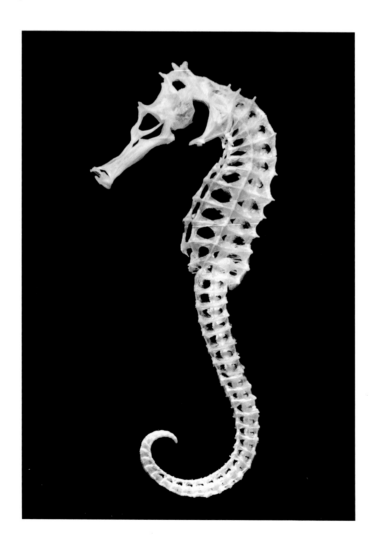

It is easy to make out the skeletal structure of this Spiny Seahorse with the skin stretched over the strong, bony frame.

Fused jaw

Seahorses, like their Syngnathid relatives the pipefish and seadragons, have a tube-shaped snout with a small mouth-like opening at the end. We can think of it as like feeding through a straw and means that they are limited to small prey. The family name Syngnathidae comes from the Greek words 'syn' meaning fused and 'gnathus' meaning jaws.

A hunting seahorse positions itself at the edge of cover, anchored by its tail to a fixed object such as a seagrass shoot, adjacent to open ground where prey gather. The seahorse leans out into the path of passing prey and singles out an individual, focusing with its chameleon-like eyes. It then sucks in the prey, swallowing it whole. With no teeth and no stomach, the seahorse needs an almost constant supply of food passing through its digestive system.

A Spiny Seahorse waits to ambush its prey on the edge of an open patch in a seagrass meadow – typical hunting territory.

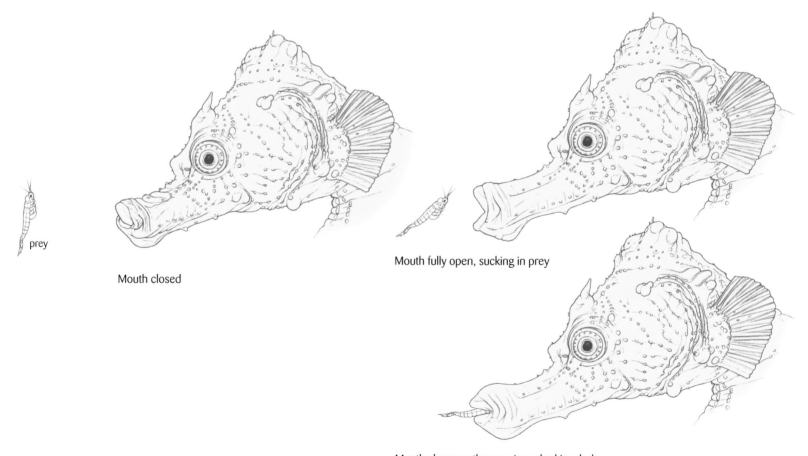

prey

Mouth closed

Mouth fully open, sucking in prey

Mouth closes as the prey is sucked in whole

Sexing seahorses

The Syngnathidae family of seahorses, pipefish and seadragons are unique in the animal kingdom, being the only species in which the males give birth. Sexing seahorses is easy because the males have a brood pouch between the bottom of the abdomen and the tail. When the male is pregnant this pouch appears swollen, especially if he is close to giving birth. At other times the pouch is still visible but more streamlined.

In female seahorses the absence of a brood pouch means their rounded abdomen ends abruptly where the tail begins and is the only visible difference between sexes. This makes the tiny anal fin, marking the junction between abdomen and tail, more visible in females. The female's ovipositor, used to implant her eggs in the male's pouch, is also close to the anal fin.

A female seahorse with rounded abdomen ending abruptly at the tail. Once the female has deposited her eggs in the male's pouch, she takes no further role in the rearing of her offspring.

A male seahorse displaying the brood pouch. Male pregnancy is unique to the Syngnathidae family.

Young seahorses

Once newborn seahorses have left the safety of the father's pouch they join the plankton to drift and feed in the surface waters. They look like miniature adults, already with the distinctive seahorse shape. Here they can feed on microscopic zooplankton, but they in turn are preyed upon by larger animals. Measuring just a few millimetres long, this is the most vulnerable time for seahorses and most will not survive to the next stage in their life cycle.

For those that do survive, the next stage is to settle on the seabed in a suitable habitat. In our experience, juvenile seahorses display the same behaviour as adults, using their tail to anchor themselves and relying on camouflage. The smallest juvenile seahorse we have encountered was just 3cm long.

A small juvenile anchored to a Sand Mason tube in an old Lugworm hole.

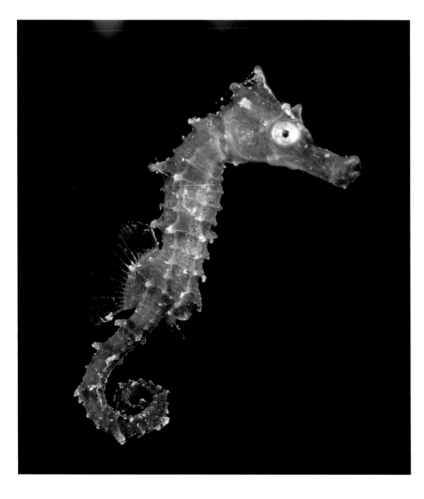

A tiny seahorse fry. At this vulnerable age the juvenile seahorse drifts in the plankton and most fall prey to larger animals.

LIFE CYCLE

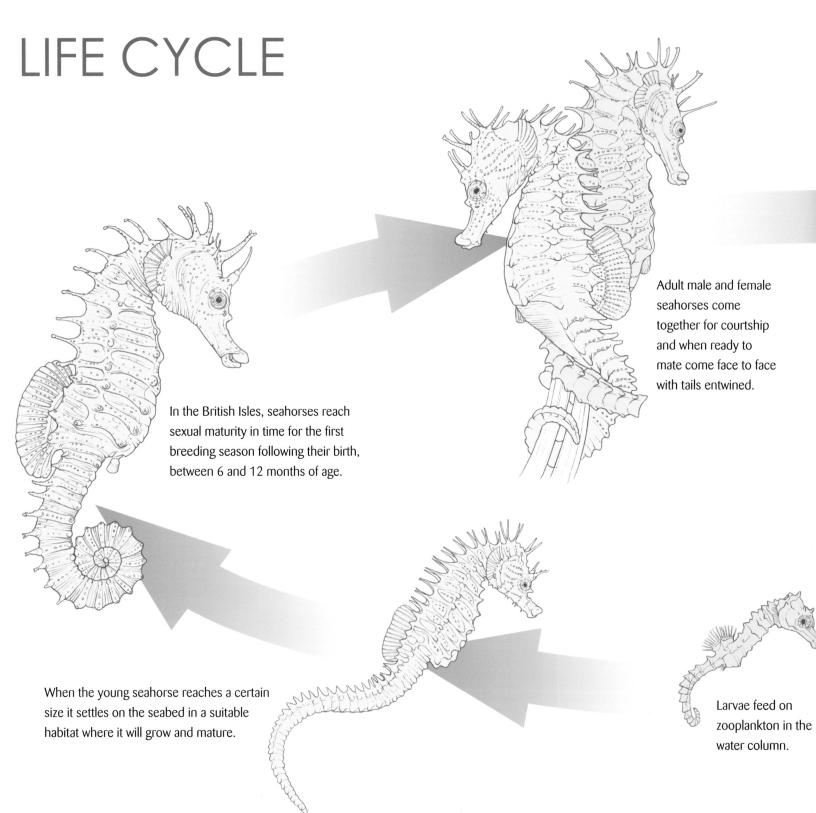

Adult male and female seahorses come together for courtship and when ready to mate come face to face with tails entwined.

In the British Isles, seahorses reach sexual maturity in time for the first breeding season following their birth, between 6 and 12 months of age.

When the young seahorse reaches a certain size it settles on the seabed in a suitable habitat where it will grow and mature.

Larvae feed on zooplankton in the water column.

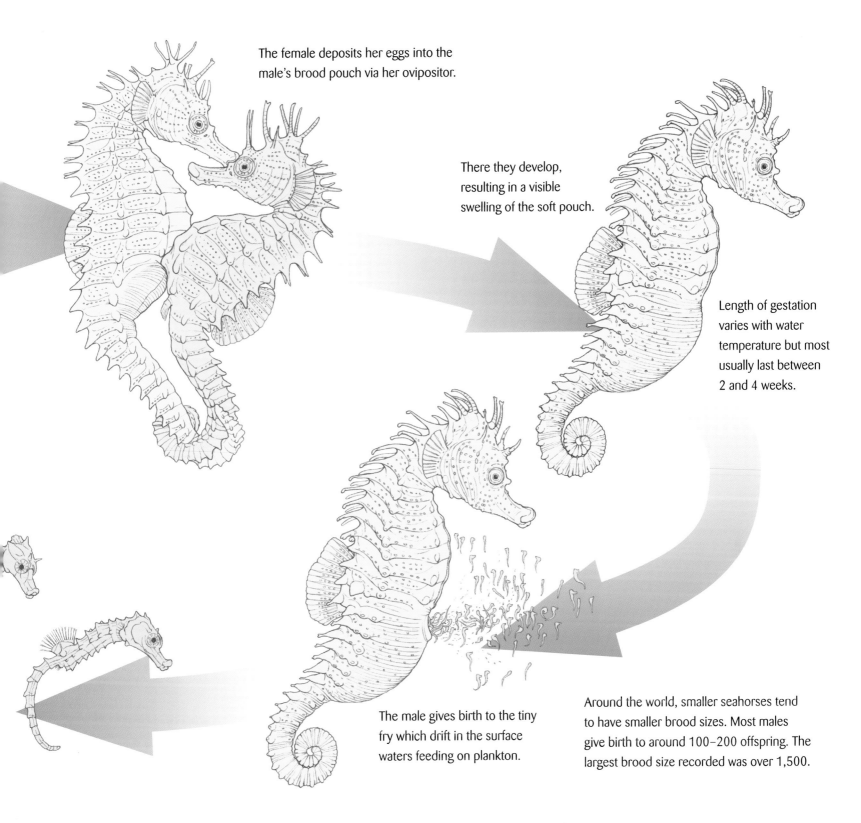

The female deposits her eggs into the male's brood pouch via her ovipositor.

There they develop, resulting in a visible swelling of the soft pouch.

Length of gestation varies with water temperature but most usually last between 2 and 4 weeks.

The male gives birth to the tiny fry which drift in the surface waters feeding on plankton.

Around the world, smaller seahorses tend to have smaller brood sizes. Most males give birth to around 100–200 offspring. The largest brood size recorded was over 1,500.

Seahorse courtship

For most seahorse species, breeding pairs remain faithful to each other throughout the breeding season. During this time the pair forage independently within a small territory and each day come together for a courtship ritual to reaffirm their bond.

We have been privileged to witness the rarely seen and very secretive pair-bonding of Spiny Seahorses. This daily ritual is an elaborate ballet in which they entwine their tails and pirouette, sometimes facing each other and sometimes facing away, with an equine tossing of their heads. This goes on for around 15 minutes or so during which they stay very close, frequently touching their bodies together and changing colour. It all happens within the secrecy and safety of dense seagrass and afterwards they each go their separate ways.

During pair-bonding, the male and female remain in close bodily contact as they pirouette, sometimes back to back as in this photograph, and sometimes face to face.

These photographs were taken one morning and it was the only time we witnessed this behaviour. Great care was taken to avoid disturbing the pair and interrupting the ritual. The secrecy of the seahorses, tucked away in dense seagrass, made observation and photography challenging.

Seahorse reproduction

In all species of seahorse, the father carries the developing eggs inside his specialised pouch. When the female is ready to transfer her eggs to the male, the pair come belly to belly and she inserts her ovipositor into his pouch. Once the eggs are implanted, the male fertilises them and the pregnancy begins.

In many ways the male's pregnancy is similar to that of mammals, where the developing young are provided with all the nutrients and oxygen they need within the relative safety of a womb or pouch. Depending on water temperature, pregnancy is between two and four weeks in duration and males can have several broods during a season.

A beautiful male Spiny Seahorse during the early stages of pregnancy, with his brood pouch clearly displayed.

Giving birth

Towards the end of pregnancy the male's pouch becomes visibly swollen. The fluid inside gradually becomes more saline to acclimatise the developing young to seawater. Most seahorses give birth to between 100 and 200 offspring per pregnancy, although this varies between individuals and species.

During labour, which happens over a period of several hours, the father releases batches of newborn seahorses by pumping and squeezing his pouch. Once born, the young seahorses have to fend for themselves with no further care from their parents.

This expectant male, in the later stages of pregnancy, is carrying the developing offspring inside his swollen brood pouch.

A TALE OF TWO SPECIES

One day we encountered the strange sight of a male Short-snouted Seahorse and a female Spiny Seahorse with their tails intertwined. We had been spotting seahorses on every dive and, while kitting up in the car park on a perfect summer's day, had been full of anticipation about witnessing something new. What we saw, however, was completely unexpected and to this day remains a bit of a mystery. The Short-snouted male appeared flushed as if taking part in a courtship ritual. Nearby was a male Spiny Seahorse. Had the Short-snouted male become confused, or were these two a breeding pair? As far as we know there is no hybridisation between seahorse species, although their ranges can often overlap. This encounter changed the way we dived with seahorses. Instead of just spotting seahorses we started to slow down and spend more time studying their behaviour.

An astonishing sight. The male Short-snouted Seahorse is flushed pink as it courts the yellow female Spiny Seahorse with their tails entwined.

CAMOUFLAGE

Seahorses are masters of camouflage. By remaining hidden and blending in, they are in a position to ambush tiny prey venturing within their reach. Slow movement also confuses potential predators, even when on open ground. Seahorse movement mimics the swaying and drifting algae around them.

The colour of a seahorse's skin is variable and depends largely on its habitat, as it has the ability to change colour to blend in with its surroundings. Spiny Seahorses living in seagrass can be yellow, olive green, brown and varying shades in between. The mane of fleshy tassels which give the Spiny Seahorse its name serve to break up its silhouette, disguising its body-shape and outline from passing predators.

This photograph illustrates how easy it is to overlook seahorses in their habitat. The fleshy spines of this individual disrupt its outline to help it blend perfectly with the surrounding seaweed.

Seahorses often lie prone on the seabed and sway with the movement of the vegetation around them.

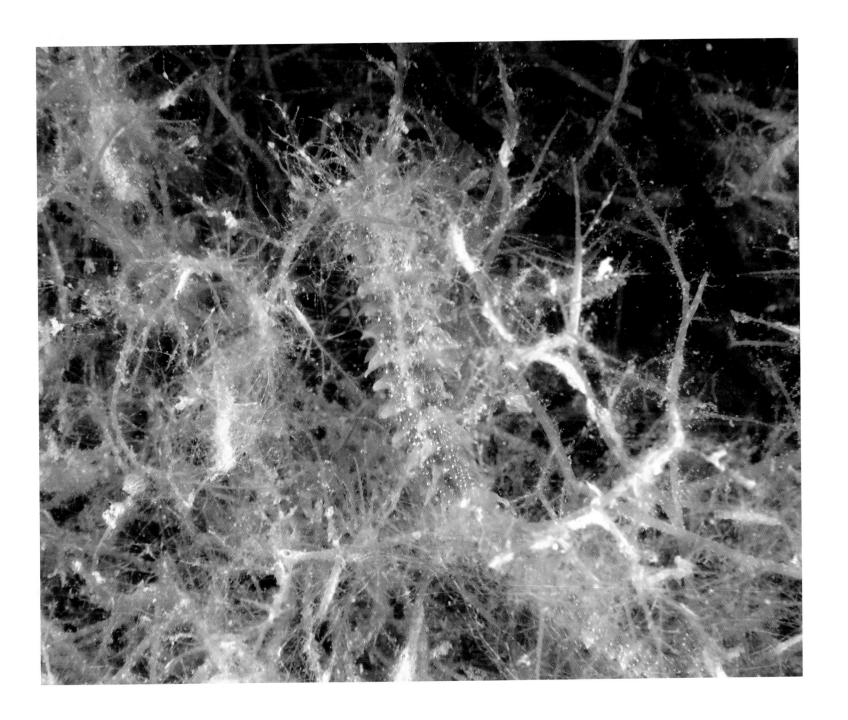

Behavioural camouflage

However good your camouflage, making eye contact immediately marks you out as an animal. Displaying false eye markings and having eyes that blend in with body camouflage are common strategies in the animal kingdom to confuse predators and prey. On many occasions, while observing seahorses in the field, we have noticed that they avoid eye contact by gradually turning their back. This also serves to disguise their shape and reduce their profile to a potential predator. Once the danger has passed they will often turn back around and continue as before.

Typically, when first encountered a seahorse will turn its head away, until it feels the threat has passed.

SEAHORSE PREDATORS

It is generally believed that seahorses are not targeted by any particular species. In fact, the main predator of adult seahorses is probably humans. Their cryptic camouflage and behaviour enables them to live side by side with potential predators in relative safety. However, they are taken opportunistically and have been found in the stomachs of large fish. Large numbers of seahorse fry have been found in the stomach of a Pollack, for example. Crabs can also take seahorses, while seabirds such as gulls have been known to pluck them from the shallows, later dropping them inland. There are records of seahorses being found in people's gardens and even in a school playground.

The most vulnerable stage of a seahorse's life is when it is newly hatched, feeding and drifting in the plankton. It is estimated that only 1% will survive this stage to settle on the seabed.

At first glance seahorses may look the same, but each has its own characteristics, like this dark-faced individual. Variable cryptic coloration enables seahorses to avoid being targeted as a prey species.

SEAHORSE PREY

Having no teeth and only a narrow mouth, seahorses are restricted to preying upon tiny animals. They mainly feed on crustaceans, but will also target fish fry shoaling in the seagrass. They are opportunistic feeders, taking whatever swims by, as long as it is small enough. As well as catching animals such as mysid shrimps (see page 160) from the water column, they pick amphipods and other tiny invertebrates from the seabed.

Seahorses have an inefficient digestive system and need an almost constant supply of live food. Seagrass beds are a highly productive habitat supporting an abundance of invertebrate prey, making them ideal for foraging seahorses. This high productivity occurs during the summer months and coincides with the seahorse breeding season.

A Spiny Seahorse leans out from the seagrass, scanning its surroundings for prey.

An amphipod, a typical component of the seahorse diet.

STRANDED SEAHORSES

Seahorses are sometimes found stranded on the beach. This may be as a result of being caught and dropped by seabirds, or being brought ashore by wave action. Seahorses are not strong swimmers and furthermore, sometimes anchor themselves to loose seaweed. Living in shallow water, it is inevitable that during rough weather some will be caught out and washed up onto the seashore.

While most strandings sadly result in death for the seahorse, live animals have occasionally been found and returned to the sea. Unlike most fish, dead seahorses do not normally rot on the beach. Instead they desiccate, retaining their shape and appearance. For very fresh strandings it may be worth holding the seahorse in a bucket of seawater for a while as it may still be alive and able to recover. On more than one occasion, a seemingly dead seahorse has survived – they can be more robust than they appear.

A freshly stranded seahorse on the strandline.

Steve holds a dried, stranded seahorse.

THREATS

Traditional Chinese Medicine

On a global scale, wild seahorse populations are under threat for a number of reasons. By far the biggest threat comes from the traditional Chinese medicine trade, which takes tens of millions of seahorses each year. They are believed to be effective as an aphrodisiac, as a growth promoter in children and as a substitute for Botox, as well as a cure for a wide variety of ailments. As a result of the belief in their health-giving properties, they are also widely eaten in Asia as a tonic. While the true number used in this trade is unknown, it is undoubtedly on an unsustainable level for seahorse populations.

Dried seahorses for sale in a Chinese market.

Curios and the aquarium trade

Over a million seahorses are taken from the wild each year to fuel the marine curio and aquarium trades. The curio trade takes live seahorses and dries them out to be sold as souvenirs, decorations for the home and jewellery. In fact seahorses form just part of a massive global trade in a variety of marine creatures, from shells and starfish to turtles and shark jaws.

The aquarium trade removes wild seahorses and exports them live all over the world for private and public aquaria. While some fish are relatively easy to care for in captivity, seahorses, with their requirement for a constant supply of live food, are notoriously difficult to keep. Only a small proportion of those taken will even survive the journey. Thankfully, there are now a number of captive breeding programmes for seahorses that supply to the aquarium trade, so that responsible aquarists can keep seahorses without impacting on wild populations.

A depressing selection of marine curios available to buy around the world.

Habitat loss

Seahorses are found in a variety of habitats worldwide, but populations tend to be concentrated in shallow, coastal seas where they inevitably come into conflict with people. Activities such as coastal development, boating, trawling and dredging have a massive impact on the coral reefs, seagrass beds and mangroves where seahorses live. Pollution from rivers and agricultural run-off from land is also concentrated in these areas. In addition to these losses, during the 1930s a wasting disease wiped out many seagrass beds around the British Isles.

It is estimated that globally, up to 50% of seagrass beds have been lost in the last 50 to 100 years, and they continue to decline.

Exposed roots around the edge of a hole in a seagrass meadow made by an anchor (see page 74).

SEAHORSE HABITATS

Worldwide, seahorses are mainly found in shallow, sheltered and highly productive habitats such as coral reefs, seagrass meadows and mangroves. In the British Isles the two species of seahorse can coexist, but differ in that the Spiny Seahorse is found almost exclusively in seagrass, whereas the Short-snouted Seahorse lives in a wider range of habitats, often at greater depths. Many of the records for Short-snouted Seahorses come from commercial fishermen who occasionally bring them up in nets and shellfish pots. The seabeds they are fishing range from sand and gravel to rocky reefs, and from estuaries and harbours to shipwrecks.

Spiny Seahorse with loose algae and Snakelocks Anemones in a seagrass meadow.

Short-snouted Seahorse amongst algae on a rocky reef.

SEAGRASS

A marine flowering plant

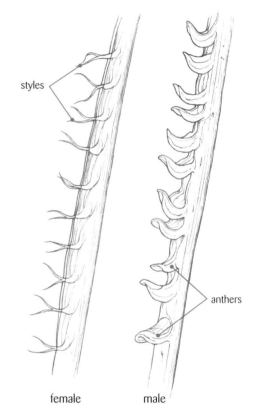

styles

anthers

female   male

Flower parts

Seagrasses are the only type of flowering plant to live totally submerged in the sea and they can form extensive meadows on the seabed in shallow water. In the British Isles, the main type of seagrass we find is called eelgrass, with two species, Narrow-leaved Eelgrass, *Zostera marina* and Dwarf Eelgrass, *Zostera (Zosterella) noltei*. Unlike seaweed, seagrass has roots and produces seeds. It grows in shallow, sheltered, sunlit waters on sandy seabeds where its roots can penetrate, forming a thick mat beneath the surface.

The leaves, looking like tall grass, can measure over 1m in length, and form a dense covering on the sea floor, giving it the appearance of an underwater meadow. Seagrass also extends into the intertidal zone where it is exposed at low tide. The flowers are inconspicuous, producing what are believed to be the longest pollen grains in the world. Pollination occurs with the help of water currents and results in seeds which are distributed by the sea.

The metre-high fronds of *Zostera marina* form a dense meadow on the sea floor.

The flower of *Zostera marina*.

Underground roots

Seagrass produces an extensive system of roots forming an interlocking mat beneath the soft sand in which it lives, and this has a variety of functions. The roots spread horizontally by producing rhizomes from which new shoots can sprout, which means that plants can reproduce asexually, in effect producing genetic copies of themselves. Plants growing in this way can reach incredible ages, even dating back thousands of years. The roots also serve to anchor the vegetation in the soft sand and trap more sand from the water column, building up and stabilising the seabed where they grow. Like all plant roots, those of seagrass store and provide the plant with nutrients absorbed from the sediment.

leaf blades

longitudinal leaf veins

mature seeds

rhizome

ligules

leaf sheath

rhizome nodes with root cluster

roots

Seagrass structure

A small island of seagrass adjacent to the main bed, helping to stabilise the mobile sand.

Coastal defence and carbon sink

Like sand dunes, seagrass meadows are one of the finest natural coastal defences we have. The dense meadow of leaves absorbs wave energy in the shallow water, reducing it before it hits the shoreline. It also traps suspended sand, building up the seabed where it grows. In this way, seagrass beds protect the coastline against erosion and flooding.

Around the world, seagrass meadows are important in slowing down the speed of climate change by absorbing large amounts of CO_2 (carbon dioxide) from the sea. Just like plants on land, CO_2 is used in photosynthesis, trapping carbon and locking it away. The sea is then able to absorb more of this greenhouse gas from the atmosphere. The rates of carbon sequestration and storage by marine ecosystems such as seagrass meadows may be higher than those of tropical rainforests on land.

A healthy seagrass meadow can lock away more CO_2 than the equivalent area of tropical rainforest.

Carbon dioxide (CO_2) released into atmosphere

CO_2 CO_2 CO_2

CO_2

CO_2 CO_2

Carbon dioxide (CO_2) dissolves into seawater

CO_2 CO_2

Seagrass takes in CO_2 during photosynthesis

O_2

C   C

Carbon (C) is locked away in plant structure, particularly roots : Oxygen (O_2) is released

Seagrass meadow traps sediment burying plant material

An important nursery

Seagrass meadows are recognised as key habitats for juvenile fish and other marine life. Being highly productive, they offer an abundant and reliable source of food as well as shelter from predators among their dense leaves. The young of a host of species, such as Bass, Pollack, Black Seabream, Sole and Plaice, inhabit seagrass beds during this vulnerable stage of their life, before venturing further afield as adults. Seagrass beds are also recognised as an important nursery for rays, including the endangered Undulate Ray, while Common Cuttlefish use them both for breeding and as a nursery for their young, which hatch there and feed upon a diet of small fish and crustaceans. For many species, which are already under pressure from fishing activity, these nursery areas are significant in providing a sanctuary while they grow.

A juvenile Pollack patrols the edge of the seagrass never far away from cover.

Sandy seagrass beds provide security for juvenile flatfish when camouflaged at rest and when they venture out from the substrate to feed.

Seagrass strandline

Seagrass grows in spring and summer, when the sunlight is strongest, and dies back a little in winter, when some of the leaves turn brown and break off, washing up on adjacent beaches. Seagrass leaves form an unusual strandline, the dead leaves drying and turning papery when washed ashore. Successive tides can push this strandline up the beach, forming folds as each new deposit is added at the seaward side. Eventually, the material will be buried in wind-blown sand where it acts like an underground 'grow-bag' for pioneer dune plants. As this fore-dune is formed it protects the dunes behind from erosion. On beaches that are mechanically cleaned, this material is removed, halting the natural process of dune formation and potentially causing the acceleration of coastal erosion. As well as providing vital nutrients for beach plants, this seagrass strandline also creates an important habitat for invertebrates such as Sand Hoppers, *Talitrus saltator.*

Folds of stranded seagrass will break down to provide the nutrients for pioneering dune plants.

Detritivores such as Sand Hoppers help to break down plant material and release the nutrients.

Human impact

Seagrass comes under threat from a number of human activities. These can be direct impacts such as removal of habitat for coastal development or indirect, such as a deterioration in water quality. The construction of hard coastal defences, reclamation of land for building, port and harbour activities and creation of marinas can all result in the loss of seagrass beds. Increased sedimentation from agricultural run-off and channel-dredging, along with a reduction in water quality through input of nitrates and phosphates, has an indirect impact on the health of the plants. It restricts their ability to photosynthesise and grow and weakens their resilience, making them more susceptible to disease.

The decline or loss of a seagrass bed results in an equivalent impact on the whole community of wildlife dependent upon it.

This female Spiny Seahorse and a whole community of companion species, including fish fry, depend upon the health and continued existence of the seagrass meadows.

A boat marina built in a harbour can impact on underwater habitats.

As seagrass beds tend to occur in shallow, sheltered bays and estuaries, they inevitably come into conflict with recreational boating activity. Traditional chain moorings consist of a heavy base on the sea floor and a metal chain reaching up to a buoy at the surface. At low tide the chain drags on the seabed and swings round like the hands of a clock as the tide rises and falls. This constant movement scours the seagrass, creating a bare circle around the fixed point of the mooring, with no opportunity for recolonisation.

A boat anchor embedded in a seagrass meadow.

Anchors are designed to dig into soft seabeds and in a seagrass meadow this means penetrating the root mat. When the anchor is retrieved it lifts the plants up by the roots, leaving a hole in the underwater meadow. During the process, anchors can be dragged, ploughing a trench through the carpet of rhizomes and leaving roots exposed. Currents then erode the loose substrate from the surrounding habitat, leaving nowhere for the horizontal rhizomes to spread.

Heavy boating activity in shallow water can suspend sand particles in the water column, reducing clarity and therefore light penetration, which limits photosynthesis. In shallow water there is also the danger of boats running aground or resting on the seabed at low tide.

Human leisure activities can inadvertently damage valuable seagrass meadows.

Heavy fishing gear towed across the seabed is an obvious threat to sensitive habitats. Scallop dredges are heavy metal cages with a rake at the front designed to displace scallops partially buried in the substrate, while a beam-trawl is a large weighted net. Multiple scallop dredges can be towed on either side of a fishing boat. The weight and spread of these types of fishing gear dragged across the seafloor have a devastating impact on seabed habitats and communities, indiscriminately catching both target and non-target species. They leave a trail of destruction in their wake and in sensitive seagrass beds, cause an additional problem by lifting the sediment, reducing the water clarity and light penetration needed for photosynthesis.

Heavy metal scallop dredges towed through sensitive seagrass meadows have a devastating impact on the habitat.

A King Scallop, *Pecten maximus*, exposed in a seagrass bed at low tide.

SEAWEED

Seahorses in the British Isles are not restricted to seagrass meadows. We know of sightings of Spiny Seahorses in harbours amongst a variety of mixed bushy algae of different heights and types, but also on pebbles and on Slipper Limpet beds in fairly sparse short, red algae. Short-snouted Seahorses are found on a wider range of substrates. We have seen one amongst seaweed-covered boulders in an area of short, red algal turf mixed with bryozoans, and know of others found on a mixed seabed of pebbles and shells with red algae. While seahorse sightings outside of seagrass meadows tend to be random, it appears that Short-snouted Seahorses are more likely to be found around the open coast and Spiny Seahorses in harbours and sheltered areas.

A Spiny Seahorse amongst sea lettuce, a green alga.

Like seagrass, seaweeds provide anchorage, shelter and camouflage for seahorses.

SOFT SEDIMENT

There are regular sightings of seahorses from areas with sand and gravel sea floors, places that are usually lacking in seaweed and indeed any kind of plant or animal cover. These are mostly encounters of Short-snouted Seahorses, although they can include Spiny Seahorses as well, and come from a variety of sources including fishermen who pull them up attached to fishing gear and divers on shipwrecks. We know that their close relatives, the Greater and Nilsson's Pipefish (see page 92), also inhabit this type of ground, but due to the cryptic character of seahorses and the random nature of sightings we have little knowledge about why they find these habitats suitable. We must assume that they are able to find a good supply of the small prey that they require.

A Short-snouted Seahorse camouflaged against sparse red algae in an otherwise open habitat.

Seahorses are regularly sighted in relatively bare areas such as this seabed habitat of loose sand and gravel with a turf of sparse red algae and bryozoans.

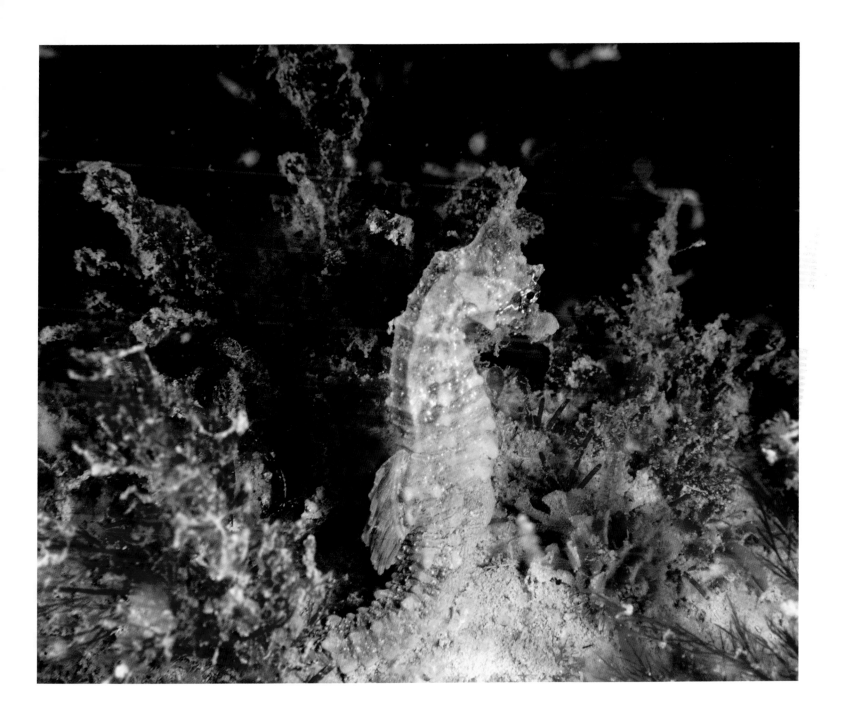

IN THE COMPANY OF SEAHORSES

Seahorses do not live in isolation but are a component of a whole community of marine life. Each species has its role to play in this interactive neighbourhood, whether it be as predator or prey, as an ecosystem engineer (burrowers and builders) or a detritivore, consuming dead material and returning nutrients to the ecosystem. There are a myriad of animals that accompany seahorses in their underwater realm. When considering the conservation of seahorses it is essential that this whole community is included, as one cannot survive without the others and a delicate balance needs to be kept. A simple overturned cockle shell, for example, will provide cover for a small goby and an anchorage point for anemones and algae, which in turn provide cover for seahorses and their mysid prey, food for sea snails and attachment for hydroids. Without Netted Dog Whelks there would be no hermit crabs, which are important both as scavengers and as food for rays. If one component is removed, the delicate balance is upset in subtle ways that are not always obvious and can be difficult to predict.

A magnificent male Spiny Seahorse in the kingdom he shares with a diverse and delicate marine community.

PIPEFISH

There are six species of pipefish in the British Isles, five of which can be found in the same habitat as seahorses. The exception is the Worm Pipefish, which is normally found in rockpools. They all belong to the Syngnathidae, the same family of fish as seahorses. The scientific name for this group refers to their fused jaws which form a tube-like mouth, while their English name describes their long, thin bodies. Like their seahorse relatives they are all experts at camouflage, sitting hidden amongst the algae or seagrass in which they live, or floating in the current like a piece of drifting vegetation. Pipefish are enclosed in a cage-like skeleton which provides rigidity and gives some an angular outline, while others are smoother in appearance.

Males carry the developing eggs beneath their body, some enclosed in a brood pouch and others in a groove. The young hatch directly into the sea and join the plankton for a time. As pipefish have tiny mouths, their diet is restricted to plankton, small crustaceans and fish larvae.

A Greater Pipefish demonstrates cryptic coloration and the unmistakable sinuous pipefish shape as it swims amongst algae on the sea floor.

A Broad-nosed Pipefish mimicking swaying blades of seagrass.

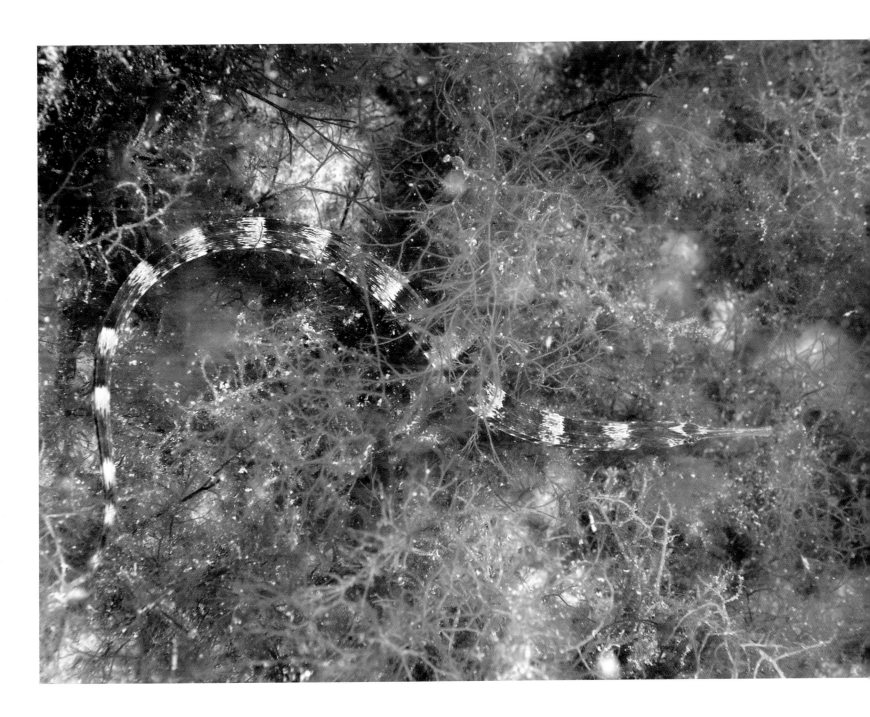

Greater Pipefish
Syngnathus acus

Size 50cm

The Greater Pipefish is one of the largest and most commonly seen pipefish in the British Isles, found in a variety of habitats. It can be identified by its angular outline and banded pattern, long snout and a distinctive hump on its head, similar to the coronet of a seahorse. Males have a brood pouch to carry the developing eggs, which may be deposited there by more than one female. The young leave the pouch when they hatch.

Greater Pipefish are found all year round in coastal habitats that include seagrass beds, rocky reefs, estuaries, open sand and amongst algae, in fact almost anywhere. They are not highly mobile and tend to stay put when approached, secure in their camouflage (see page 85).

A Greater Pipefish showing its long, tube snout. The tiny mouth is right at the end.

Snake Pipefish

Entelurus aequoreus

Size 60cm

This is the longest of all the British pipefish and one of the most widespread. Its English name describes its long, snake-like body, smooth in outline with a distinctive pattern of pale rings on a copper-coloured background. A darker stripe runs through the eye along the side of the head and snout. Unlike the Greater Pipefish this animal has a prehensile tail with the tail fin almost absent. The tail is used to anchor the animal by wrapping around fixed vegetation. Males lack the brood pouch of some pipefish, instead having an open groove in which to carry the eggs. Snake Pipefish can be found in a variety of habitats including seagrass, estuaries and on mixed ground amongst seaweed.

In the early 2000s there were reports of an abundance of Snake Pipefish around the country, with photographs of puffins unsuccessfully trying to feed them to their chicks. To help with research we carried out some sampling in our local area and counted 71 in a small area of seagrass meadow – an astonishing number. Over subsequent years the numbers declined again.

A Snake Pipefish exhibits a series of pale rings around the thin body and the characteristic dark eye-stripe.

A prawn net pushed through seagrass in the early 2000s revealed Snake Pipefish in unusual abundance.

Broad-nosed Pipefish
Syngnathus typhle

Size 35cm

The Broad-nosed Pipefish is mostly found in seagrass beds, to which it is supremely adapted. Its name derives from the shape of the snout, which appears as deep as the head and body. It is generally coloured green or mottled brown to blend in perfectly with the seagrass stems (see page 84) and it habitually swims in a vertical position to complete the camouflage. We have witnessed brown individuals disguised as a broken-off piece of dead seagrass frond and swimming across the seabed as if they are being gently swept to and fro by the current. We have also seen an individual drifting just inches below the surface of the sea in open water, holding a vertical position and looking just like a piece of the drifting seaweed that accompanied it.

Broad-nosed Pipefish males take the care of their young a step further than other pipefish. They have a brood pouch into which a number of females may deposit their eggs. Once hatched, the youngsters can return to the safety of the pouch if they feel threatened.

Close up of a Broad-nosed Pipefish snout displaying its ability to blend in with the seagrass amongst which it lives.

A surprising encounter with a drifting Broad-nosed Pipefish at the surface of the open sea.

Nilsson's and Straight-nosed Pipefish
Syngnathus rostellatus and *Nerophis ophidian*

Sizes 17cm and 30cm

The Nilsson's Pipefish is a small species that could easily be mistaken for a young Greater Pipefish, although on close inspection it lacks the bump on the head and only reaches about one-third of its maximum size. We have learned to recognise Nilsson's Pipefish because of where we find them, typically on the open sand. They often shelter where loose algae collects in hollows left by lugworms or other burrowing creatures, or behind ripples in the sand.

    The Straight-nosed Pipefish has a distinctive snout which is short, but appears as wide as the head. Although widespread, it is one of the most secretive of pipefish and is rarely seen by divers. It is found mainly in seagrass beds or dense algae, and for camouflage has a green or brown coloration, lighter on the sides and with vivid electric-blue markings along the head and body. It lacks a tail fin and instead has a prehensile tail. Males do not have a brood pouch but carry the eggs in a groove beneath their body.

A Nilsson's Pipefish in its typical habitat on the open sand.

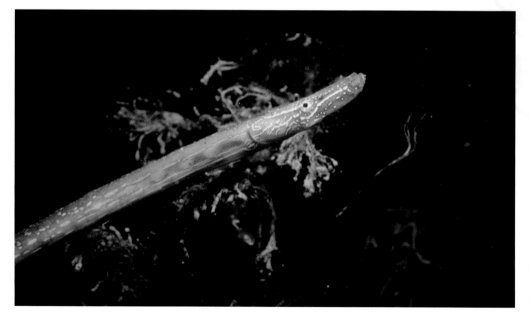

A Straight-nosed Pipefish displaying its iridescent markings and distinctive snout.

STICKLEBACKS

Fifteen-spined Stickleback
Spinachia spinachia

Size 15cm

The Fifteen-spined Stickleback is a common shallow-water fish with a distinctive torpedo shape, found among seaweed in rocky areas and seagrass on sandy seabeds. As the name suggests, it has a series of spines along its back. It has superb camouflage and amongst seagrass, displays a bright green coloration. The colour and shape work to give it the appearance of a blade of seagrass and by keeping still amongst the fronds, it can become all but invisible. These fascinating fish are difficult to observe but are always encountered in the upper canopy of the underwater meadow and rarely in the open.

A male Fifteen-spined Stickleback builds a nest by wrapping fine, silvery threads he produces himself around bundles of seaweed. When a female has laid her eggs inside, he fertilises them and then tends the eggs until they hatch. These fish spawn only once and both male and female subsequently die.

A Fifteen-spined Stickleback imitating the shape, colour and angle of a blade of seagrass.

Observing Fifteen-spined Sticklebacks in seagrass is difficult. If you take your eye off them for a second they just disappear as if capable of invisibility.

RAYS

Undulate Ray
Raja undulata

Size 100cm

The Undulate Ray is one of a number of ray and skate species found around the British Isles. Unlike some of its ocean-dwelling counterparts, however, this species is mostly found inshore in relatively shallow water and as such can be found among seagrass meadows as well as on sandy and rocky seabeds in shallow water. It is a more southerly species, at the northern edge of its range along the south and south-west coasts of England. It is easily distinguished from other rays by its striking pattern of wavy lines edged by pale spots.

Rays belong to the same group of fish as sharks and have a skeleton made of cartilage instead of bone. Members of this group, called the elasmobranchs, are relatively slow to mature and produce a much smaller number of young than bony fish. For this reason they are very susceptible to overfishing and the Undulate Ray is now classified as Endangered on the IUCN Red List of Threatened Species.

The patterns on an Undulate Ray, outlined with rows of white dots, are reminiscent of Aboriginal art.

Undulate Rays lay their eggs on the seabed in which a single developing embryo feeds on a yolk. When sufficiently developed they hatch out of the egg, measuring 14cm long, fully formed and able to fend for themselves. The discarded eggcases can wash up on to beaches and are known as mermaid's purses, along with those from other species of shark or ray.

Through a combination of mermaid's purse surveys and photographing juveniles on the seabed we have been able to identify a nursery area for this species in Studland Bay, Dorset. Seagrass meadows are recognised as providing nursery habitat for fish, offering shelter and an abundance of food in the form of mysid shrimps and similar small crustaceans which are the staple food of juvenile Undulate Rays.

This juvenile Undulate Ray measured about 15cm across the wings and, unusually, had algae growing from the spines along its back.

A hatching Undulate Ray emerges from its eggcase with its wings folded over its body.

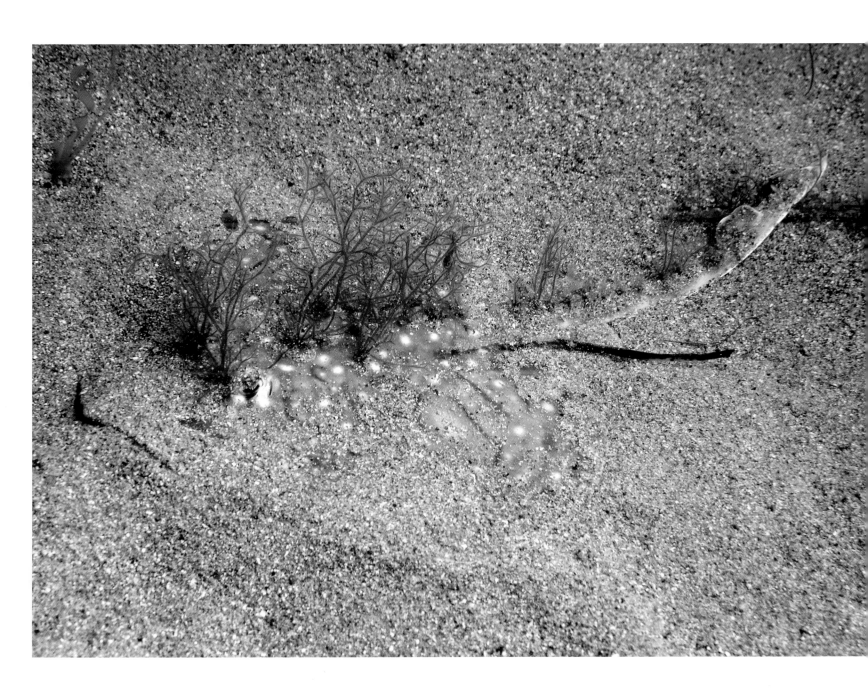

FLATFISH

As a group, flatfish have evolved to lie on the seabed and are adept at camouflaging themselves. To achieve this they go through a type of metamorphosis to change from normal upright-swimming fish as planktonic larvae to lying on their side as an adult. The change is completed by their lower eye migrating so that both eyes are on the top side. For most flatfish the eyes are on their right side but a few have their eyes on the left.

Flatfish are very important commercially and include species such as Plaice, Sole, Turbot and Halibut. Seagrass beds are recognised as important nursery areas for the juveniles of many types of flatfish. Almost all prefer soft seabeds where they are able to completely cover themselves in a thin layer of sand, remaining hidden with just their eyes exposed.

Flatfish often hide beneath a fine covering of sand.

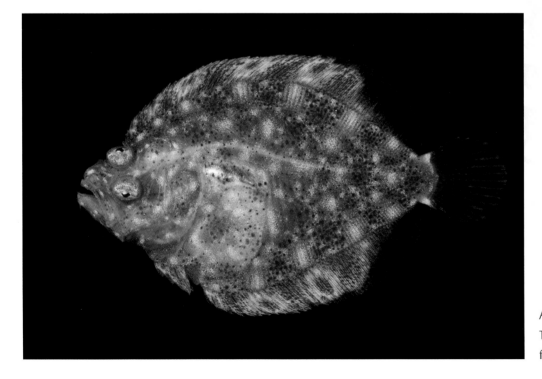

At a mere 5mm long, this planktonic Turbot has already transformed, ready for a life on the seabed.

Plaice

Pleuronectes platessa

Size 50cm

The Plaice can be identified by the orange spots on the top (visible) side of its body, although these are not always obvious. It is one of the most commercially important flatfish and overfishing has resulted in a reduction in its size. Whereas Plaice once measured up to 1m in length, they now rarely exceed 50cm.

Plaice tend to be more active at night, feeding on molluscs, shrimps and worms on the seabed. These animals feel so secure in their camouflage that it is easy to get close and observe them as they lie in the sand, without them swimming away.

Plaice have the lopsided face characteristic of flatfish, as a result of one eye migrating to the other side of the head during the larval stage.

Plaice are ambush predators, lying camouflaged on the seabed awaiting their unsuspecting prey.

Dab and Sole

Limanda limanda and *Solea solea*

Size 40cm (both)

The Dab is very similar in appearance to the Plaice but lacks the orange spots, making it drabber in colour and with a more curved lateral line. The Sole, also called the Common or Dover Sole, has a different outline, making it easier to distinguish from other flatfish. It is more slipper-shaped, with a curved head and a frilly beard. Like other flatfish, the Sole no longer reaches the large sizes that it once did, and nowadays rarely exceeds 40cm in length. In seagrass beds these two species are normally encountered as juveniles rather than adults, confirming that this type of habitat is important as a nursery area.

The skin of this Dab perfectly matches the colour of the sand where it lives.

The Sole has a distinctive rounded head with a short, frilly beard.

The fleshy spines of Spiny Seahorses can vary greatly from very long, branched and abundant to short, sparse and simple.

This particular seahorse was seen amongst sea lettuce and a hair-like alga that was particularly abundant one year, occurring possibly as a result of heavy rain and freshwater run-off.

GOBIES

Black Goby
Gobius niger

Size 17cm

Despite its English name, this stout goby is very rarely black, most commonly being grey with pronounced dark blotches along its flanks. Other identifying features are rows of sensory black bristles on its head and a large, almost triangular dorsal fin which it usually holds erect. It inhabits sandy areas and is common in seagrass beds, where it lives in shallow burrows beneath stones or shells. We even observed a resident Black Goby living underneath a discarded frying pan on the sea floor. They do not tend to stray far from their burrow and will dart back under cover if threatened.

A Black Goby displaying its large first dorsal fin.

A Black Goby peeps out from its burrow, ready to retreat to safety if threatened.

Two-spot Goby
Gobiusculus flavescens

Size 6cm

The Two-spot Goby is named for the two dark spots on each side, which makes it unmistakable among gobies. Its behaviour also distinguishes it from its relatives; it swims in the water column rather than down on the seabed. The only exception is during the breeding season when males descend to the sea floor to guard their eggs. In seagrass meadows Two-spot Gobies gather in small shoals, patrolling the edge of the habitat where they feed on planktonic shrimps and larvae. In summer, clouds of juveniles can be seen and are prey for seahorses and other seagrass inhabitants.

This Two-spot Goby, on the seabed surrounded by a colony of Horseshoe Worms, *Phoronis hippocrepia*, is possibly guarding eggs.

Unlike most gobies, Two-spot Gobies typically swim in the water column.

Sand, Common and Painted Gobies
Pomatoschistus minutes, P. microps and P. pictus

Size 6cm (all)

Small gobies are notoriously difficult to identify, the Sand and Common Gobies particularly so. Both the latter species can be abundant on sandy seabeds and in seagrass meadows but are incredibly difficult to photograph, darting away before you get close enough. They lack any distinguishing markings and are a plain, sandy colour. They are slender, delicate-looking fish that live on the seabed, darting around feeding on tiny worms and crustaceans disturbed from the sand. Male Sand Gobies sometimes have a small, dark mark on their first dorsal fin which can be seen if held erect.

Painted Gobies are easier to distinguish, as they have pale blue markings on their dorsal fin and flanks and are altogether more patterned, with dark blotches along their sides. They tend not to be seen in the same numbers as the Sand and Common Gobies.

The top photograph shows either a Sand or Common Goby; they are difficult to tell apart in the field. The bottom photograph is of a Painted Goby with characteristic pale blue markings on the dorsal fin and flanks.

WRASSES

Corkwing Wrasse
Symphodus melops

Size 15cm

The Corkwing Wrasse is commonly seen in a variety of shallow-water habitats, especially amongst seaweed and in seagrass beds. A dark spot on the tail stalk is a characteristic feature and distinguishes it from other wrasse species. Corkwing Wrasse are residents in seagrass beds but may move to deeper water in the winter months. Juvenile fish tend to hide in the denser stands of seagrass for protection. These fish mainly feed on small crustaceans such as crabs and shrimps.

Males build and decorate an elaborate nest out of loose seaweed in spring and early summer. They select particular types and colours of seaweed, hoping to attract females to lay their eggs. Several females may lay eggs in a male's nest, which he then fertilises. He will remain with the nest, tending and caring for the eggs until they hatch. During the breeding season the males are territorial and will defend their patch, boldly swimming up to divers and other fish that encroach.

The black spot on the tail stock is an identifying feature of the Corkwing Wrasse.

A Corkwing Wrasse devouring a mysid shrimp.

Ballan Wrasse
Labrus bergylta

Size 60cm

The Ballan Wrasse is the largest of the wrasse species in the British Isles. Adults sport a variety of colours and patterns, from plain to mottled, pale to dark brown and even bright red with white spots in some older fish. Juvenile Ballan Wrasse are often a uniform emerald-green colour. While Ballan Wrasse inhabit a variety of marine habitats, those living in seagrass beds are mostly the green juvenile fish, which use it as a nursery area and are well camouflaged against the green seagrass.

These fish all start life as females, with a proportion of the population changing sex to become males. They feed mainly on crustaceans and molluscs and have an extra set of teeth in their throat to crush the hard shells of their prey. These throat or pharyngeal teeth are referred to as a Ballan Cross and were once treasured by sailors as a good luck talisman.

Adult Ballan Wrasse are found in a wide array of colours from lime green, as here, to brown or red, with pale spots.

An emerald-green juvenile Ballan Wrasse hides amongst dense seagrass.

OTHER FISHES

Sea Scorpion
Taurulus bubalis

Size 25cm

This fish is a master of camouflage, changing its colour to blend in with whatever habitat it is living in. Commonly found in seagrass beds, it also lives in a wide range of other shallow-water habitats. It is an ambush predator, lying motionless until something tasty swims by, at which point it will lunge forward to engulf its prey. Its large mouth enables it to take animals almost as big as itself. Despite its name and appearance, this fish is not venomous, although it has spines on its cheeks resulting in an alternative name of Long-spined Sea Scorpion. Similar-looking scorpion fish from the same family are venomous, although these are rare in inshore waters.

The Sea Scorpion is the ultimate ambush predator, lying motionless and confident in its camouflage.

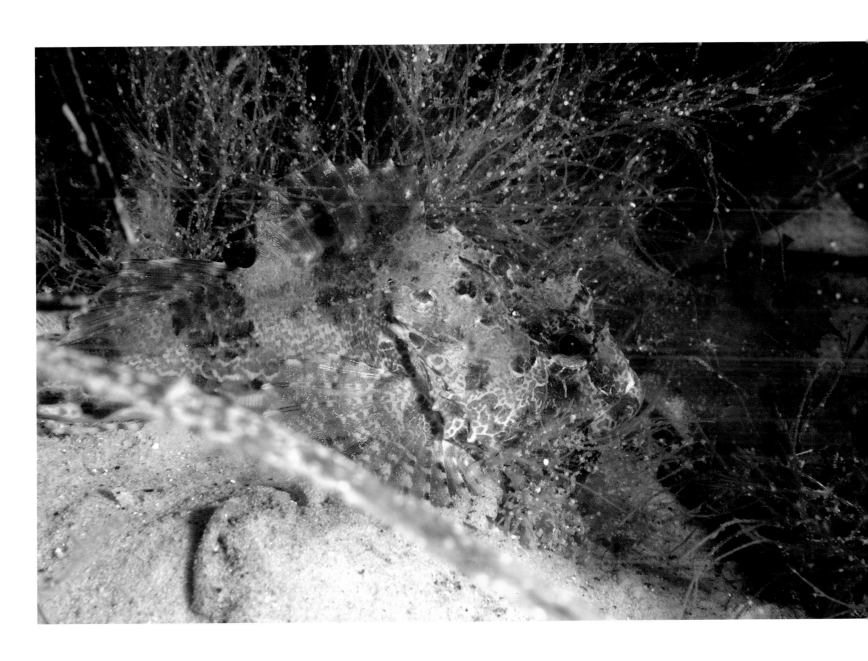

Black Seabream
Spondyliosoma cantharus

Size 60cm

The Black Seabream is a deep-bodied, silvery fish. Breeding adults aggregate in specific locations to excavate shallow, crater-like nests in which to lay their eggs, with the males remaining to tend and protect them until they hatch. Juveniles are commonly found in seagrass meadows, an ideal habitat and vital nursery area providing cover from larger predators whilst supplying a copious amount of food for the growing fish. Amongst their favoured foods are young cuttlefish, another seagrass inhabitant. The juvenile fish, measuring up to around 5cm in length, tend to hang out at the edge of the habitat but are shy of divers, ready to retreat into the dense cover of the seagrass blades if threatened. We have never seen adult Black Seabream in seagrass meadows.

A juvenile Black Seabream scouting around the edge of a seagrass bed, ready to retreat to safety at the first sign of danger.

Bass

Dicentrarchus labrax

Size 1m

The Bass is a beautiful fish, streamlined and silvery. It is an active and voracious predator and young Bass, normally found in small groups, give the impression that they are hunting for prey like a pack of wolves. Small shoals of sub-adults are frequently seen patrolling above the seagrass canopy. They feed on fish such as sand eels, juvenile Pollack and Sand Gobies, either taken in the water column or directly from the seabed. Seagrass meadows are important for young Bass, as they provide an abundance of the small fish prey they require.

We have witnessed seahorses out on open ground seemingly unconcerned by shoals of Bass patrolling overhead. Presumably the seahorses' slow or stationary demeanour does not attract attention from these high-speed hunters.

Large, mature Bass like this one tend to be more solitary than younger individuals.

Pollack

Pollachius pollachius

Size 130cm

The Pollack is a member of the cod family but lacks the typical chin barbel and has three triangular dorsal fins that are very distinctive. As an adult it is commercially fished, growing to over 1 metre in length, living in deeper water. At this stage it is often found around shipwrecks or on rocky reefs, where it feeds on smaller fish such as sand eels. As a juvenile it is much more colourful and inhabits shallow-water nursery areas amongst seaweed and seagrass, where it hides from predators while feeding up on small crustaceans and fish. When it moves out of these nursery areas the colour will change to a plain, steely grey to better blend in with its deeper, less colourful habitat.

A colourful juvenile Pollack in its nursery area.

Red Mullet
Mullus surmuletus

Size 40cm

The Red Mullet is one of our most colourful fish, with boldly marked scales. It exhibits a deep red pattern with yellow and pale blotches at night, but during the day, and in shallower water, it becomes paler with darker stripes along its sides. It has a pair of chin barbels used to sense prey buried beneath the surface of the sandy seabeds where it lives. The barbels are in constant motion, like fingers probing in the sand for crustaceans and worms. Upon finding something, this fish uses its blunt head to uncover its quarry, which produces a cloud of sand. Juvenile Red Mullet can often be seen in small groups in seagrass meadows.

A Red Mullet probing the seabed with its sensory barbels. Juveniles often form part of the seagrass meadow community.

Lesser Weever
Echiichthys vipera

Size 15cm

The Lesser Weever is one of the few venomous fish found in British waters and inhabits sandy seabeds, where it spends the day buried with just its eyes showing. For this reason it is one of the most feared by holidaymakers and surfers entering the sea. However, the fish is not actively aggressive and only stings as a last resort when in danger. When disturbed, it emerges abruptly from the sand, erecting a black dorsal fin as a warning as it darts away. If accidentally stepped on it can inject venom through its spines, and anyone who has been stung in this way will know it is an incredibly painful and unforgettable experience. The Lesser Weever is more active during the night and can be present in large numbers. It has an upturned mouth, making it easier to catch prey that unwittingly wanders close enough, although at night it will also feed in the water column, targeting shrimps and small fish such as gobies.

By day a Lesser Weever lies buried beneath the sand.

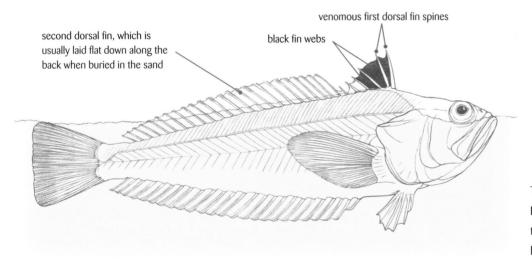

second dorsal fin, which is usually laid flat down along the back when buried in the sand

black fin webs

venomous first dorsal fin spines

This illustration reveals a view of the Lesser Weever not normally seen, as the fish spends most of its time lying hidden in the sand.

Sand Smelt
Atherina presbyter

Size 20cm

The Sand Smelt is a small, silvery-coloured, shoaling fish common in shallow waters, including seagrass meadows. During the day it feeds on plankton and other invertebrates in the surface waters, including flies trapped on the surface film. An inhabitant of warmer waters, it is found in the more southern and western areas of Britain and is one of the species sometimes referred to as 'whitebait'. On a bright, sunny day, shoals of Sand Smelt are an amazing sight as they twist and turn in the water, reflecting the silvery light. At night their behaviour is entirely different as they hang motionless in the water column, appearing almost to sleep, only darting away if they are approached.

The Sand Smelt is a slim-bodied inshore fish that swims in tightly packed shoals.

Sand eels
Ammodytidae

Size 20–35cm

Sand eels form a major part of the diet of many seabirds and larger fish. There are five species of sand eel in the British Isles, of which two are widespread: the Lesser Sand Eel, *Ammodytes tobianus*, and Greater Sand Eel, *Hyperoplus lanceolatus*. They spend their time either buried in the sand on the sea floor, or forming large, silvery shoals. Sand eels are distinctive fish with a thin, elongated body, although despite the name they are not an eel. Divers may see them as a silver flash as they shoot out of the sand when disturbed. Animals such as cuttlefish and Pollack may follow a diver, waiting for their prey to be flushed. One or two Greater Sand Eels will often be mixed in with a shoal of Lesser Sand Eels, their much larger size marking them out.

The dark mark on the snout of this fish identifies it as a Greater Sand Eel, an important prey species for seabirds and larger fish.

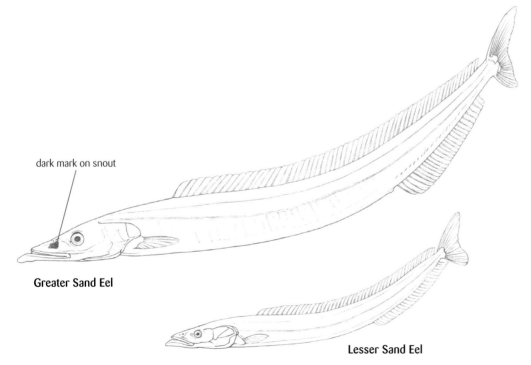

dark mark on snout

Greater Sand Eel

Lesser Sand Eel

The differences between Lesser and Greater Sand Eels

Reticulated Dragonet
Callionymus reticulatus

Size 11cm

There are several species of dragonet in British waters and all look very similar. They are not only difficult to tell apart but are also difficult to spot with their cryptic colouring and habit of sitting motionless on the seabed, or moving in short bursts as they glide over the seafloor in search of hidden prey such as worms and other invertebrates. Inhabitants of soft seabeds, their coloration is designed to mimic the shell and sand fragments in the particular area where they live, so colour can vary between locations. The Reticulated Dragonet is the one we encounter, and they can be abundant in seagrass beds. The prominent eyes on top of the head and the flattened body are reminiscent of flatfish.

The Reticulated Dragonet's colour varies to exactly match the sand on which it is found.

Despite having had dozens of seahorse encounters, the excitement of seeing a seahorse has never worn off and we are just as thrilled with each new sighting as we have always been.

Every encounter is different. Sometimes there is a particularly photogenic seahorse in characteristic side-on pose, other times it may be hidden in dense cover, or exhibiting evasive behaviour.

CRUSTACEANS

Crustaceans are a large group of mainly marine animals within the even larger group called Arthropods. They include familiar species such as crabs, lobsters and prawns. Crustaceans have a hard outer casing called the exoskeleton, which must be shed or moulted periodically as they grow. Amongst the most familiar of this group are a number of commercially valuable shellfish.

Crustaceans all have jointed legs which can be adapted for walking, swimming, fighting or feeding. There are a number of sub-groups within the crustaceans which have differing numbers of legs. Crabs, for example, have four pairs of walking legs plus one pair of claws and belong to a group called decapods.

A Common Lobster on a rocky reef, which provides holes and crevices from which it emerges to feed at night.

A freshly moulted Shore Crab alongside the shell it has shed.

Masked Crab
Corystes cassivelaunus

Carapace length 4cm

The Masked Crab gets its name from the pattern on its carapace which is said to resemble a face or mask. It spends the majority of its life concealed in the sand, but is often more active at night when it emerges to feed. Its paired antennae are edged with bristles and interlock to form a breathing tube which protrudes above the sand when the crab is buried. The crab's oval shape is designed to enable rapid burial in the sand when it is threatened. Males are easily distinguished from females by the exaggerated length of their claws, which can be used for sparring with other males.

This sequence of photographs shows the Masked Crab burying itself in the sand.

A female Masked Crab can be identified by its shorter claws.

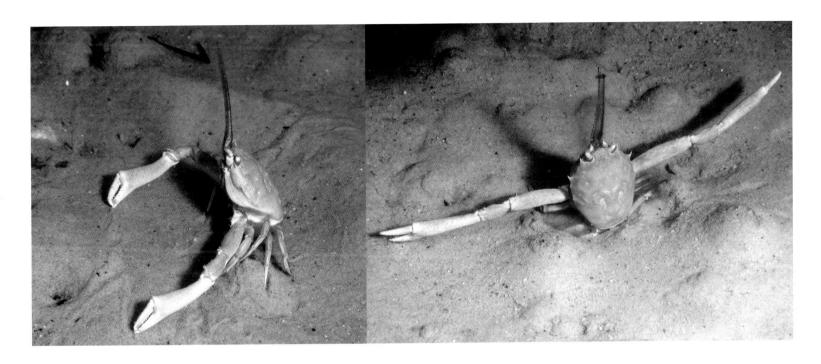

Common Spider Crab
Maja brachydactyla

Carapace length 20cm

This is one of the largest crabs in the British Isles and is easily recognised by its spiny, teardrop-shaped carapace. Common Spider Crabs have a habit of decorating their shells with seaweed or other growth in order to blend in with their surroundings. Unlike most other crabs, they are active in daylight and can be seen out in the open, although highly decorated individuals can be difficult to spot unless they move. They sometimes gather together in very large numbers to moult their shells, and these aggregations form a rarely seen wildlife spectacle. Newly moulted crabs are very quick to redecorate their shells.

An elaborately decorated Common Spider Crab in seagrass.

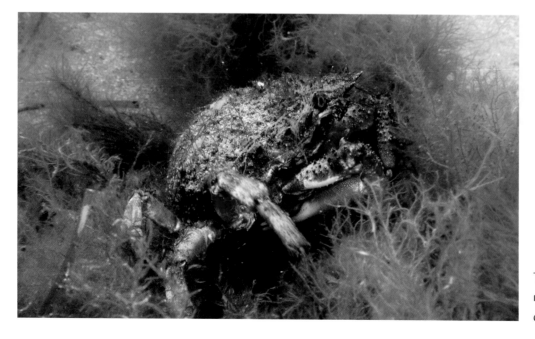

The larger Common Spider Crabs do not normally have the elaborate decoration of their younger relatives.

Long-legged spider crabs
Macropodia sp.

Carapace length 2cm

Unlike the much larger Common Spider Crab these crabs have spindly legs and tiny bodies. Nevertheless, they are normally very highly decorated with algae, almost to the point of invisibility. We have witnessed these crabs disappear before our very eyes. We watched one walk across the seabed and then step into a clump of loose seaweed and merge with it. When we examined the clump closely we found two other individuals already within.

In the British Isles there are several very similar species that are hard to identify in the field.

This individual is in a defensive posture, having been caught out on the open sand.

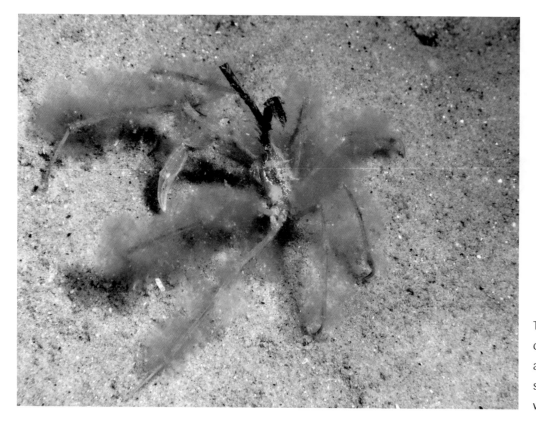

These crabs can be so highly decorated that they become all but invisible in their chosen surroundings. Only movement will give their position away.

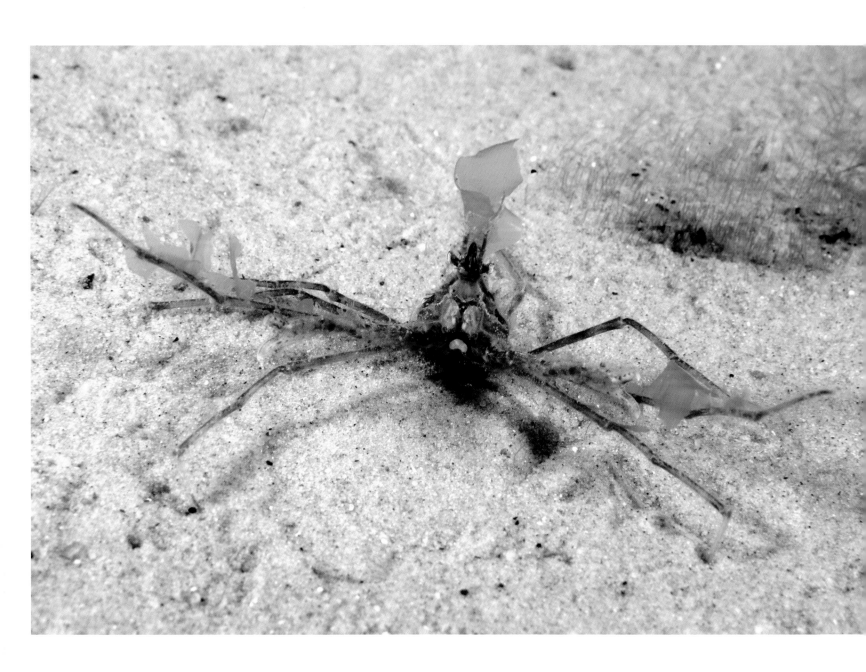

Four-horned Spider Crab
Pisa tetraodon

Carapace length 6cm

Like all spider crabs, this small crab decorates its shell with algae or other growth as a means of camouflage. It is usually spotted by accident during investigations of dense seaweed as it is never found out in the open. The males' much longer claws distinguish them from females. There is another, similar species, but this one has four distinct 'horns' between the eyes, although these may be well hidden beneath its algal covering. At first glance these crabs look like very young Common Spider Crabs, but their rear legs are noticeably shorter.

The four horns that give this crab its name are very difficult to make out as they are normally hidden beneath the crab's decoration.

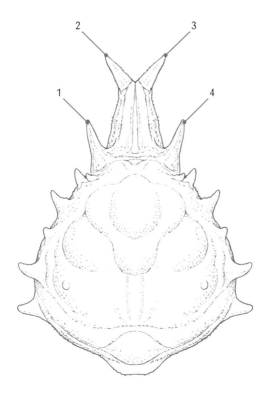

The characteristic four horns without their normal algal covering.

Harbour Crab
Liocarcinus depurator

Carapace length 7cm

The Harbour Crab is a carrion-feeding scavenger, found only on sandy seabeds, where it hides beneath the surface during times of inactivity. Its carapace is sandy coloured and its rear pair of legs are tinged a blue-purple, hence one of its alternative names: the Blue-legged Swimming Crab. As in other swimming crabs, these rear legs are flattened, enabling the Harbour Crab to swim short distances. If caught out in the open, this belligerent crab will sometimes adopt an aggressive stance with its sharply spiked claws outstretched. Alternatively, it can swim away rapidly.

A Harbour Crab devouring its mollusc prey.

Like all swimming crabs, this species is confrontational, and typically stands with claws outstretched if threatened.

Shore Crab
Carcinus maenas

Carapace length 8cm

The Shore Crab is our most commonly seen crab, found in all kinds of shallow marine habitats, from rockpools and seagrass beds to muddy estuaries. A familiar find for anyone who has ever gone crabbing or rockpooling, it has also spread around the world and can be a pest in countries where it is not native. While newly settled juveniles can exhibit a variety of shell patterns, they quickly take on the uniform green and yellow shell that give this crab the alternative name of Green Shore Crab. Older individuals have a brown and orange shell.

Shore Crabs are host to a parasitic barnacle, *Sacculina carcini*, which changes their behaviour and prevents them from breeding. The barnacle is visible beneath the tail flap of its host and could be mistaken, at first glance, for an egg cluster. However, it is smooth textured and close observation will reveal it pulsating.

The most familiar crab to anyone who has been rockpooling or dropped a crab line over a harbour wall.

The parasitic barnacle, *Sacculina carcini*, can be seen attached below the body of its unfortunate host.

Common Hermit Crab
Pagurus bernhardus

Carapace length 3cm

This is the commonest and most familiar of hermit crabs, found in rockpools as well as a variety of habitats, including sand and seagrass meadows. Hermit crabs are not true crabs, using empty sea snail shells, which they carry around to protect their soft bodies. When little, they start off in small mollusc shells such as periwinkles and topshells, moving on to larger ones as they grow, until when fully grown they occupy Common Whelk shells. If the shell is large enough to accommodate them they will disappear completely inside when threatened, slowly emerging to check if the coast is clear. Like other hermit crabs, they moult their hard exoskeleton periodically as they grow, although this is limited to their claws, legs and head as the body is soft and hidden inside the shell.

A fully grown Common Hermit Crab inside a Common Whelk shell.

A small Common Hermit Crab inside a periwinkle shell.

Small Hermit Crab
Diogenes pugilator

Carapace length 1.5cm

The Small Hermit Crab, also known as the South Claw Hermit Crab, differs from other hermit crabs in that its left claw is the larger of its two claws. It inhabits sandy seabeds in shallow water and can be very abundant. Small Hermit Crabs look comical when large numbers of them rapidly back away over the undulating ripples of sand, dragging their exaggerated left claws behind them. Like all hermit crabs this species has a soft body which it hides in empty mollusc shells. Being small, it favours the small Netted Dog Whelk shells commonly found on sandy seabeds. Small Hermit Crabs are scavengers and will often fight over the dead remains of a mollusc or other detritus on the sea floor.

The Small Hermit Crab in its typical habitat of soft sand in shallow water.

The left claw of this hermit crab is too large to tuck inside the shell and is always visible.

Anemone Hermit Crab
Pagurus prideaux

Carapace length 1.5cm

This small hermit crab has a symbiotic relationship with a species of sea anemone which grows over the mollusc shell the crab inhabits. The anemone grows to encompass the shell and beyond, creating an extension to the crab's home, hence its name Cloak Anemone, *Adamsia palliata*. The relationship benefits both parties. The anemone continues growing with the crab. The crab, protected by both the original shell and the anemone, never has to go through the stress of transferring to a bigger shell, while the anemone gains by having a regular source of food, feeding on the crab's left-overs. The anemone also protects its host by ejecting sticky white stinging threads when the pair are threatened.

The Cloak Anemone is only partially covering the shell of this Anemone Hermit Crab but defends its host by ejecting white stinging threads when threatened.

The Cloak Anemone has completely encased the Anemone Hermit Crab's shell.

Common Prawn
Palaemon serratus

Size 10cm

The Common Prawn is distinguished from other, similar prawns by its long, beak-like rostrum and is commonly found in low-shore rockpools, on rocky reefs and in seagrass meadows. It often hangs around in the entrance of crevices with lobsters and crabs and in seagrass meadows, rarely venturing out from amongst the dense vegetation. The delicate claws are used to pick detritus from other animals, algae and the seabed. This prawn will even give you a manicure if you hold your hand still, picking the dirt from under fingernails. If threatened, it darts backwards for cover with a rapid flick of its tail.

A Common Prawn forages for detritus with its tiny claws.

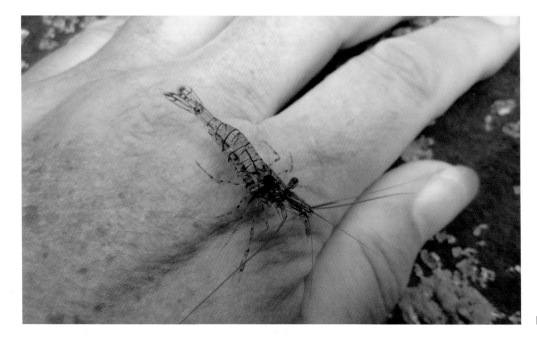

Providing a manicure service.

Mysid shrimps
Mysidae spp.

Size 1.5– 2.5cm

Mysid shrimps, also known as opossum shrimps, are a large group and most are hard to identify to species level. They are very common in seagrass meadows, where they group together into small shoals, usually sheltering close to the edge of the vegetation. They hang in the water column, and as they are almost transparent, can be difficult to spot, their dark eyes being the only feature that stands out. They are more abundant in the summer months and are probably the staple food of seahorses during their breeding season.

The alternative name of opossum shrimp comes from the pouch on the female's underside for brooding the offspring.

Mysid shrimps position themselves vertically next to cover.

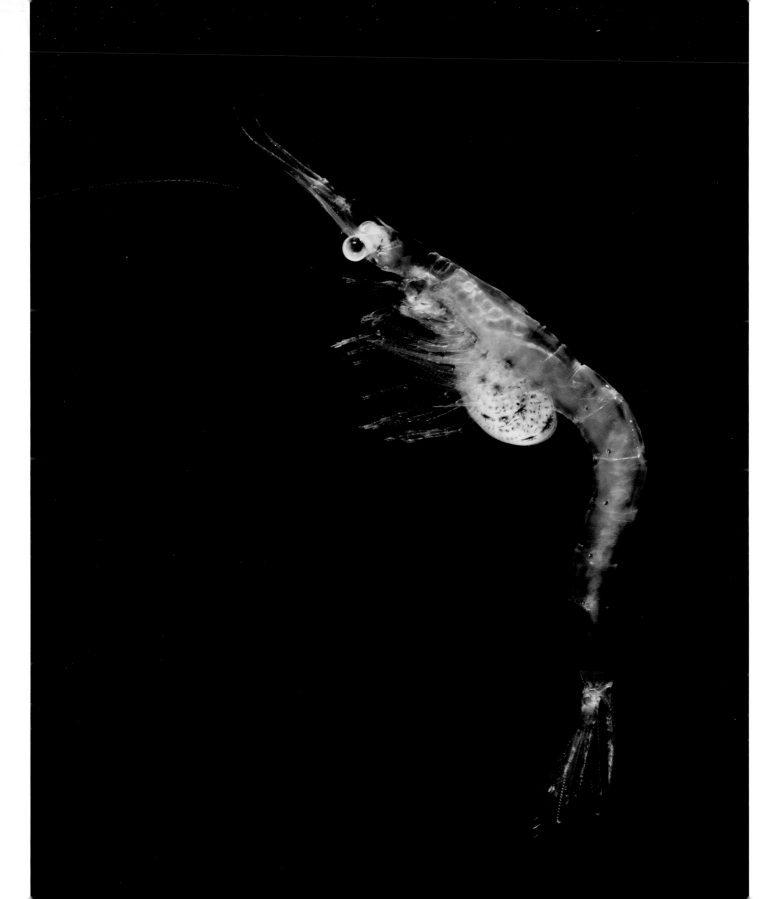

Chameleon Prawn
Hippolyte varians

Size 3cm

The colour of this prawn can be incredibly variable depending on where it is living, hence its English name. The one pictured here was found amongst seagrass but individuals living in rockpools can be pink, brown, flecked or almost transparent. Although this is a common species, Chameleon Prawns are rarely seen because of their cryptic coloration. Like all crustaceans, they moult their exoskeleton, leaving them more vulnerable until their outer layer hardens. It is likely that juveniles of this species make up part of a seahorse's diet.

An emerald green variation of the Chameleon Prawn as found in a seagrass meadow.

Moulting prawn left; newly moulted right.

Brown Shrimp
Crangon crangon

Size 8cm

The Brown or Common Shrimp is distinguished from the Common Prawn by its flattened body, which enables it to bury itself beneath sand with just its eyes showing, whereas the Common Prawn does not bury itself and has a more arched body. As a result, Brown Shrimps are only found with sand, whereas Common Prawns are more variable in their habitat. While the name may suggest that this shrimp is always brown, its colour can vary to match the sand where it lives. It emerges to feed and if threatened, can rapidly retreat beneath the surface. As well as being a commercially fished species, Brown Shrimps are an important food source for many fish and birds.

Even when emerged from its hiding place it is difficult to spot this highly camouflaged shrimp.

A Little Grebe, *Tachybaptus ruficollis*, eating a Brown Shrimp.

Anemone Shrimp
Periclimenes sagittifer

Size 3cm

In recent years the Anemone Shrimp has extended its distribution to the south coast of England, whereas previously its most northerly record was from the Channel Islands. It is a brightly coloured shrimp that would look at home on a tropical reef, with its violet leg bands and a lilac chevron on its back. Indeed, it has many tropical relatives. It lives within the stinging tentacles of the Snakelocks Anemone, *Anemonia viridis*, to which it is immune, using them for protection but seemingly offering nothing in return (see page 180). Despite its colourful markings, it is remarkably hard to spot when hidden beneath the tentacles, but by sweeping the tentacles aside it can be revealed.

The anemone's tentacles look almost like tree trunks in comparison to the diminutive Anemone Shrimp.

Isopod
Idotea linearis

Size 4cm

This marine relative of terrestrial woodlice is superbly adapted to living in seagrass meadows, although it is not restricted to them. Its brown, elongated body enables it to camouflage itself perfectly when positioned along a blade of dead seagrass with its legs wrapped around it and its long antennae folded together. We have watched these animals tumbling across the seabed attached in this way to the broken blades of seagrass and they are easily overlooked. While marine isopods are a large group, the appearance and behaviour of this one is very distinctive.

The isopod *Idotea linearis* at home amongst seagrass.

Only a keen eye will notice these small and supremely adapted seagrass inhabitants.

We have noticed that the seahorses we have encountered are often in this horizontal position, looking down at the seabed, whilst anchored by their tail. As well as feeding on prey from the water column, they also feed on tiny crustaceans on the sand.

BRISTLE WORMS

Lugworm
Arenicola marina

Size 20cm

The coiled cast of a Lugworm is a familiar sight on sandy and muddy beaches at low tide and for divers in the shallows. It marks one end of a U-shaped burrow in which the worm lives and is formed by the faecal remains of the Lugworm's meal. About 30cm away, the other end of the burrow is marked by a depression in the sand where organic material collects. The worm ingests this sand, digesting the organic material and leaving the mineral part for excretion. Lugworms can be very abundant on shallow, sandy seabeds and are an important food source for various species of wading birds and flatfish. Wading birds patrol the lower shore at low tide looking for movement as a cast is formed, curling like toothpaste squeezed from a tube. At this point the tail end of the worm is at the surface and accessible to a probing bill.

Mounds of sand on the seabed indicate the tail-end of Lugworm burrows with the tell-tale casts excreted by the worm.

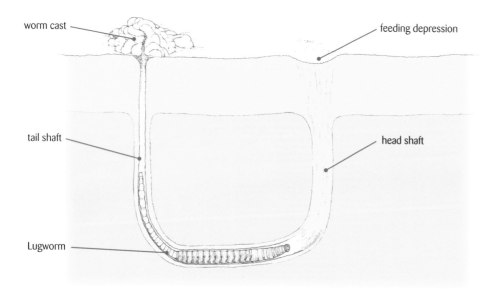

worm cast

feeding depression

tail shaft

head shaft

Lugworm

The Lugworm in its U-shaped burrow.

Eyelash Worm
Myxicola infundibulum

Size 5cm across crown

The Eyelash Worm is found in sandy and muddy areas, where it extends its funnel-shaped crown of feeding tentacles just above the surface so they lie flush with the seabed. The funnel formation is formed because the individual tentacles are joined together along their length, and the name Eyelash Worm comes from the black tips on the tentacles. Food is trapped in the fine hairs of the crown. These worms are difficult to spot as they retreat rapidly into their burrows if approached. Like many filter-feeding worms, their tentacles are very vulnerable to predation when extended out of the burrow.

A lucky shot of an Eyelash Worm's extended feeding tentacles. These are normally retracted in the blink of any eye when approached.

Sand Mason Worm
Lanice conchilega

Size 20cm

Although the worm is not normally seen, its tree-like tube, built of sand particles and shell fragments, is a common feature of sandy shallows and seashores at low tide. The worm extends its tentacles through the branches of the structure to feed and collect material to extend its tube. Mucus holds the sand grains together and gives the structure some flexibility to withstand wave action, although in rough conditions broken tubes can accumulate in great numbers on the beach strandline. On beaches where Sand Mason Worms are abundant they can look like a miniature forest on a low spring tide.

The delicate branching structure of a Sand Mason tube, through which the worm's feeding tentacles are extended.

Broken tubes washed up after rough weather.

Peacock Worm
Sabella pavonina

Size crown 15cm across

The Peacock Worm is a common inhabitant of seagrass beds but is also found in various sandy, muddy, gravelly and rocky habitats. Its tough, leathery tube can measure up to 25cm long, although in soft seabeds much of it is buried beneath the surface. Even then, the tube extends well above the sea floor, keeping the colourful but delicate crown of feeding tentacles out of the sediment. Like other tube worms, the Peacock Worm retracts its tentacles with lightning speed when sensing danger. On a number of occasions we have seen seahorses using Peacock Worm tubes as an anchorage (see page 24).

The crown of delicate feeding tentacles face into the current to trap plankton drifting by.

The leathery worm tube keeps the delicate crown clear of the seabed.

CNIDARIANS

Snakelocks Anemone
Anemonia viridis

Size 20cm

Snakelocks Anemones can be extremely abundant in seagrass meadows, where they can attach to shells and pebbles on the sand but mostly live on the seagrass blades in the canopy. For fish swimming through the dense stands they can present a minefield of stinging tentacles to negotiate. They are also common in rockpools and on rocky seabeds, where they can form 'gardens'. Sometimes several anemones close together seem to form one very large individual. This happens when one grows and divides into two, a form of asexual reproduction where clones of the original are created.

Like other anemones, the Snakelocks Anemone uses stinging tentacles to paralyse its prey. However it also benefits nutritionally from photosynthesising algae living within its body. An ultraviolet torch used at night shows that some individuals fluoresce.

A Snakelocks Anemone in the canopy of a seagrass meadow.

Some Snakelocks Anemones fluoresce under ultraviolet light.

A sea anemone
Sagartiogeton undatus

Size 12cm

This anemone is most often found on sand, where it attaches to firm objects such as stones and live mollusc shells beneath the surface. Its column is mostly buried, with just the tentacles above the sea floor. Each tentacle has a line along its length and also pale bands around it, but both disc and tentacles can look quite colourless and the anemone is therefore easily overlooked. If disturbed, *Sagartiogeton undatus* withdraws its tentacles.

This anemone is attached beneath the sand to a razor shell, whose keyhole-shaped siphon is clearly seen.

Sagartiogeton undatus

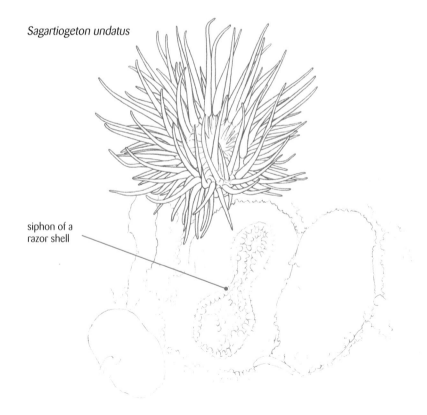

siphon of a
razor shell

Illustration to explain the
photograph opposite.

Burrowing Anemone
Cerianthus lloydii

Size 10cm

The Burrowing Anemone lives in a tube which is buried in sand or mud with the top extending above the sea floor. Instead of retracting its tentacles as some anemones do when threatened, this one withdraws its whole body into the tube. The outer tentacles are long and slender, while the inner tentacles are much shorter and densely packed around the animal's mouth. Like tube worms, the Burrowing Anemone is hard to observe as it will retract rapidly into its tube if approached.

The long tentacles encircle the crown of the anemone while the short ones surround the central mouth.

This photograph shows the sandy tube into which the entire body of the Burrowing Anemone can retract.

A sea anemone
Peachia cylindrical

Size 12cm

Sometimes known as the Clock-face Anemone, this burrowing anemone has only 12 broad tentacles, with distinctive W-shaped markings along them. These tentacles lie flat against the seabed when the anemone is feeding. Beneath the sand is a long body or column with a bulbous end which extends quite deep and anchors the animal in the soft substrate, although it does not have a tube or sheath. We have seen these anemones living in seagrass meadows.

The mouth of the anemone can be seen in the centre, surrounded by the 12 tentacles.

The distinctive broad tentacles of this sea anemone, with W-shaped patterns along them.

Stalked jellyfish
Stauromedusae

Size 2.5cm

Stalked jellyfish are members of the Cnidaria: animals with stinging cells including jellyfish, sea anemones and corals. Unlike their free-swimming cousins, stalked jellyfish, as the name suggests, attach to algae and seagrass via a flexible stalk. Their inverted umbrella, edged with stinging tentacles, is held out into the water to catch small invertebrate prey. These exquisite, star-like animals exhibit beautiful symmetry and colour, but being small, are easily overlooked.

Several different species might be encountered in the company of seahorses, including the Kaleidoscope Jellyfish, *Haliclystus auricula*, the Maltese Cross Jellyfish, *Calvadosia cruxmelitensis* (sometimes called the St John's Jellyfish), its close relative *Calvadosia campanulata*, and the vase-shaped *Craterolophus convolvulus*.

From top left: *Haliclystus auricula, Craterolophus convolvulus, Calvadosia campanulata, Calvadosia cruxmelitensis.*

MOLLUSCS

This large group of animals contains the garden snails and slugs, types of gastropod that we are all familiar with, but also some exclusively marine examples. Cephalopods are a group of highly evolved predatory molluscs found only in the sea and include the octopus, cuttlefish and squid, while bivalves are molluscs with a protective shell in two halves such as cockles and mussels. The basic body plan of a gastropod mollusc is of a soft animal enclosed in a hard shell, but many mollusc groups have evolved to reduce, internalise or altogether lose their shell, or, as in the case of bivalves, to redesign their shell into two halves connected by a hinge.

Molluscs regularly feature in our everyday lives, whether we are gardeners, seafood eaters or simply visiting the beach. Some species are of high commercial value as shellfish, and fishing for them has wrought havoc on marine ecosystems all over the world.

The octopus is regarded as one of the most intelligent of invertebrates, capable of problem-solving, and as such is probably one of the ocean's most charismatic animals.

The Common Whelk is a gastropod with the familiar spiral shell and muscular foot.

Common Cockle
Cerastoderma edule

Size 4.5cm

The Common Cockle is a bivalve that can be found in abundance living buried just below the surface in sandy and muddy sand seabeds. The two valves or halves of the shell are equal, plump and rounded, with deep ridges radiating out from the hinge. Cockles extend their siphons to the surface for feeding and respiration. The shells are iconic and recognisable symbols of the seashore, and are particularly common in estuaries and muddy bays. As well as being a commercially collected species, these animals are an important food source for wading birds. Cockles also serve as a solid anchorage for animals such as sea anemones in an otherwise shifting and fluid environment.

The Common Cockle, a familiar bivalve that lies just beneath the surface of sandy and muddy seabeds and has one one of the most recognisable shells of all molluscs.

An Oystercatcher, *Haematopus ostralegus,* prizing open a cockle at low tide.

Razor shell
Solenidae

Size up to 20cm

There are several species of razor shell, all of which exhibit the long, narrow and very distinctive shape resembling a cut-throat razor. The outer surface is covered in a flaky periostracum which looks like peeling varnish. These bivalves live buried beneath sandy seabeds in a vertical position, extending their pair of siphons to the surface. Underwater, the siphons are recognisable among other types of bivalve as they have a distinguishing keyhole shape. Razor shells are adept at burrowing down if threatened and can rapidly retreat deep into the sand using their muscular foot, liquidising the sand beneath them to make it easier. They are a commercially collected species and have been overfished in some places.

The tell-tale keyhole-shaped siphons give away the position of this razor shell buried beneath the sand.

An empty razor shell washed up on the shore, showing the two identical halves.

Fan Mussel

Atrina fragilis

Size 25cm

The Fan Mussel is the largest bivalve to be found in the British Isles. Today, it is also one of the rarest and, as such, is protected under UK law. The fan-shaped shells are thin and fragile and the animal lives buried vertically at the surface of soft sea floors with just the top few inches proud of the sand. For this reason, the exposed shell may be broken and is often encrusted in anemones and other molluscs, making it difficult to spot, especially in seagrass. The pointed lower part of the shell attaches to buried stones for anchorage, using fine byssus threads. During an official survey for this species in Devon in 2007, an exposed Fan Mussel was found lying at the surface of an intertidal seagrass bed, having been dislodged somehow. This provided an opportunity to see the live animal in all its glory before reburying it.

A Fan Mussel lies buried in a seagrass meadow at low tide with the top few inches of the shell extending above the surface.

Steve holding a Fan Mussel during an official survey.

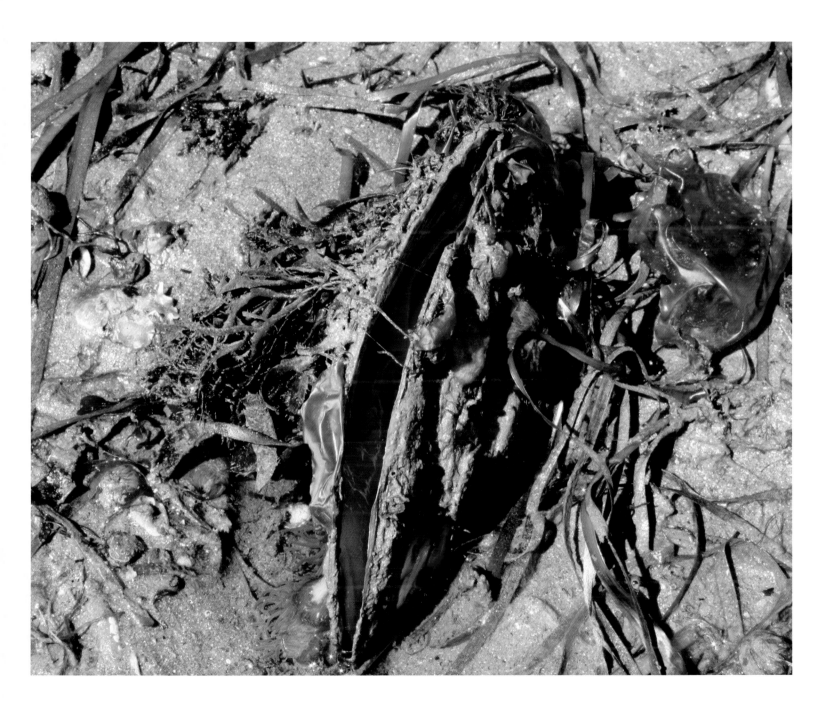

King Scallop
Pecten maximus

Size 12cm

The King Scallop, also called the Great Scallop, is a bivalve that lives on the surface of soft seabeds. Probably the most recognisable of all shells, it has been used as a symbol for centuries – from the fine art of Botticelli's 'The birth of Venus' to the logo of a global oil company. While scallops can be found in deeper water, they also live in shallow water and intertidal seagrass beds. The two valves are unequal, one being curved while the other is flat. When at rest, they lie with the curved side down, the two shells partly open to reveal rows of blue eyes. If threatened by a potential predator such as a starfish, scallops can flutter away for a short distance by clapping their two valves together.

A King Scallop lies agape with its many tiny eyes keeping watch for any approaching danger.

The iconic shape of the King Scallop has been used as a symbol of the sea for centuries.

Netted Dog Whelk
Tritia reticulata

Size 3cm

This small gastropod hides beneath the sandy sea floor, erupting from the surface at the first hint of something dead or dying on which it can feed. It extends its long siphon in front to 'smell' the water and follow the chemical scent to its target. Large groups of Netted Dog Whelks appear to gather from nowhere to feed on carrion and when finished, they disappear again beneath the sand. The shell has a chequered pattern and will often be inhabited by small hermit crabs once vacated by its original owner. This humble snail is a very important component of the ecosystem, helping to break down and recycle dead matter. The Netted Dog Whelk lays its eggs in rows of little oval flasks attached to algae and seagrass blades.

A group of Netted Dog Whelks congregate to feast on a dead razor shell.

Netted Dog Whelk egg capsules laid along a seagrass blade.

Icelandic Cyprine
Arctica islandica

Size 11cm

The Icelandic Cyprine is a large, robust, deep-bodied clam which lives buried in seabeds of muddy sand. It has a dark skin or periostracum, which becomes flaky and peels off when shells are washed up. Its round to oval shell exhibits a series of very fine concentric rings, one for each year of growth, which means that individuals can be aged. The oldest known Icelandic Cyprine was nicknamed Ming and collected from the seabed during a survey. It was found to be 507 years old and there may be even older ones in the wild. While they are found in deeper water, Icelandic Cyprines can also be seen in shallow coastal water and are sometimes present in seagrass meadows.

A rare sighting of the Icelandic Cyprine's robust shell lying exposed on the seabed.

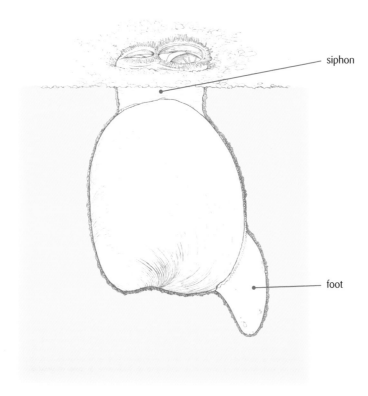

siphon

foot

The Icelandic Cyprine in its normal position beneath the sand, with only the siphons visible.

Tiny sea snails

Rissoa parva, Lacuna parva, L. vincta, Tricolia pullus and *Hydrobia* spp.

Size under 1cm

Some of the most abundant animals in both seagrass and weedy habitats are tiny molluscs measuring under 1cm in length. They are difficult to identify and photograph in the field, being so small, although sweeping a net through weed will often reveal them. These snails graze on the fronds and leaves in great numbers, digesting the vegetable matter and transferring it up the food chain by becoming prey for fish and other animals. Although tiny (the Latin name 'parva' means tiny), they are a vital component of the whole ecosystem. The eggs of the Least Chink Shell, *Lacuna parva*, laid in rings on the leaves and fronds of its host, are very distinctive, looking like tiny, green doughnuts.

Clockwise from top left: Pheasant Shell, *Tricolia pullus*; Least Chink Shell, *Lacuna parva*; *Rissoa parva*; *Hydrobia* sp.; *Hydrobia* sp.; *Rissoa parva* with eggs.

Necklace Shell
Euspira catena

Size 3cm

This animal is also known as the Moon Snail and is a predatory gastropod, its globular shell is partially covered by its white mantle when the snail is active. The Necklace Shell lives in sandy seabeds, where it ploughs through the surface, preying on bivalves buried there. To extract the soft animals from their shells it drills a hole near the hinge using its hard radula. Eggs are laid in a collar-like structure made of mucus and sand grains, each egg sitting in its own little pit.

A second, smaller species, the Alder's Necklace Shell, *Euspira nitida*, is very similar and lives in the same type of habitat. The egg mass of this species forms a complete and overlapping ring.

A Necklace Shell glides across the seabed on a muscular foot with its white mantle partially covering the shell.

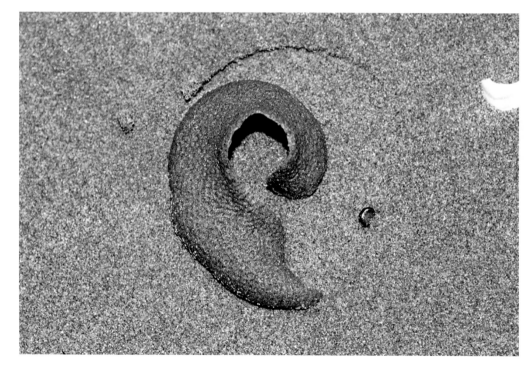

The mucus and sand egg collar of the Necklace Shell washed up on a beach.

Sea Hare

Aplysia punctata

Size up to 20cm

The Sea Hare, a type of sea slug, sometimes gathers in large aggregations in shallow waters to breed. The name derives from the long sensory tentacles on the head, which give it a hare-like appearance. It is a herbivore, feeding on algae, from which its colour derives. The smaller *Elysia viridis*, usually found on green algae, has the added benefit of hosting algal cells in its body. These trap sunlight to produce energy from which the slug profits, like a built-in solar panel. A third species, *Aplysia fasciata* is much larger, growing up to 40cm in length and weighing almost 2kg.

Sea Hares are hermaphrodites, forming mating chains for breeding where each individual acts as both male and female to the individuals either side of it in the chain. When disturbed, they can discharge an unpleasant purple fluid to deter predators. Pink or orange eggs are laid in long, intertwined strands.

A Sea Hare's sensory tentacles are reminiscent of a hare's long ears.

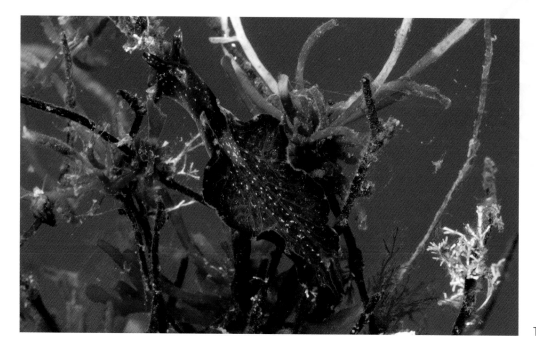

The small, solar-powered *Elysia viridis*.

Common Cuttlefish
Sepia officinalis

Size 30cm

Common Cuttlefish are dynamic, fascinating and intelligent animals and are a favourite of divers for many reasons. They have often followed us on dives, hovering beside us, curious to see what animals we might disturb or uncover, in the hope of an easy meal. They belong to the cephalopods along with the octopus and squid, a group of highly evolved molluscs that are active and highly mobile predators.

Cuttlefish use stealth and camouflage to sneak up on or ambush their crustacean and fish prey, shooting out a pair of long, extendable tentacles tipped with sucker-covered paddles to catch them and pull them in. A sharp, parrot-like beak is then used to crush and dismantle them while they are held in the grip of the eight remaining suckered tentacles. The crunching of shells and bones can be heard by divers who witness this spectacle.

These animals are prey to a number of large fish and marine mammals and are equipped with a variety of escape strategies. If threatened they can rapidly retreat, using a siphon to jet propel themselves backwards whilst releasing a cloud of ink as a smokescreen. The brown ink, called sepia, has been used by people for centuries and gives the cuttlefish its scientific name.

Common Cuttlefish are masters of disguise, able to instantly change both the colour and texture of their skin to hide from predators and ambush prey. They also use this ability for communication during courtship, at which time they produce shimmering patterns of stripes across their bodies to woo partners while also warning off rivals.

A Common Cuttlefish waits for the photographer to flush its prey from the seabed.

Common Cuttlefish congregate in coastal waters during spring and summer to breed. They lay clusters of eggs which they attach to seaweed, seagrass or man-made pots and ropes. The eggs, sometimes called sea grapes, are round and black and contain ink to hide the single embryo inside. On hatching, the newborn Cuttlefish are about the size of a salted peanut and are already efficient predators, capable of fending for themselves.

The adults only breed once and then die, having put all their energy into producing the next generation. The soft tissue of their bodies quickly decays, leaving just the hard cuttlebone, a structure which is used to provide buoyancy. These wash ashore in large numbers and can be found in a wide variety of sizes on beach strandlines.

As the Cuttlefish is now a target species for commercial fishing, the importance of nursery areas, where the young can feed and grow rapidly, has never been greater. Seagrass meadows provide just such an area, with an endless supply of mysid shrimps, small crustaceans and juvenile fish to supply its voracious appetite.

Tiny Cuttlefish use seagrass meadows as a nursery area while they feed and grow.

A bunch of sea grapes, the ink-filled eggs of a Cuttlefish.

Little Cuttlefish
Sepiola atlantica

Size 5cm

The Little Cuttlefish is one of our favourite marine animals and it is always a delight to see them. Finding one can be difficult, however, as they are experts at camouflage and bury themselves beneath the sand, usually with only their large eyes showing. If disturbed, they shoot out of the sand, leaving a little puff of ink to screen their escape, only swimming a few metres before burying themselves again. This they do by using their tentacles to sweep sand over their bodies, and once they have finished, they clear their eyes by wiping two tentacles across like a pair of windscreen wipers in the most endearing way.

Like their larger cephalopod relatives, Little Cuttlefish have the ability to change colour instantly by expanding or contracting specialised cells in their skin called chromatophores to reveal or conceal pigment.

The plump and compact Little Cuttlefish has to be one of the cutest molluscs you can encounter on a dive.

The thumbnail-sized Little Cuttlefish are highly efficient predators like their larger relatives, and can instantaneously change colour to match their surroundings.

While most of the seahorses we have seen have had a clean outline, occasionally we have come across some with a fine dusting of silt trapped on the fleshy spines and tubercles of the body, like the one pictured on the right.

ECHINODERMS

Sea Potato
Echinocardium cordatum

Size 10cm

The Sea Potato is also called the Heart Urchin and is indeed a type of sea urchin. The body is enclosed in a hard but fragile 'test' or shell which in turn is covered in bristles, some of which are used to aid burrowing. Living in sandy seabeds, the Sea Potato first ploughs a furrow in the sand, excavating a burrow angled downwards until it is buried beneath the surface. It then extends long tube feet up to the depression at the entrance to the burrow where food collects.

Often the only indication of this animal's presence is when stormy conditions cause large numbers of the empty tests to wash up on to the beach. Although very fresh ones may still have the bristly coat attached, most are found as clean, white and often broken shells.

A rare view of a live Sea Potato with its test covered in bristles.

The delicate test from a dead Sea Potato that has lost its bristles.

Serpent Star
Ophiura ophiura

Size 25cm

The Serpent Star is a large, active brittlestar that lives on the surface of sandy seabeds, and is normally covered with a light dusting of sand. Brittlestars are radially symmetrical, with five bristly arms radiating from a small central disc which contains the mouth and forms the main part of the body. The arms are used to transfer food to the mouth on the underside of the central disc. As the English name for this group suggests, the arms are brittle and easily broken if handled, although they can regenerate. The Serpent Star's arms are relatively short; only four times as long as the diameter of its broad central disc. It uses them to move rapidly across the sea floor.

A solitary Serpent Star moving across the sea floor.

Sand-burrowing Brittlestar
Acrocnida brachiata

Size 40cm

All that is normally seen of this brittlestar are the tips of some of its long arms sticking up above the sand. They are often in large aggregations, with numerous spindly arms protruding, trapping passing plankton in their bristles. By gently fanning the sand away the whole animal can be revealed, with its small central disc and long, curly arms.

The normal view of these animals is a forest of thin white arms protruding from the seabed.

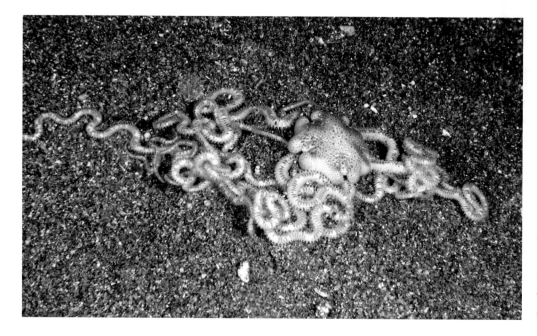

An exposed Sand-burrowing Brittlestar reveals its exceedingly long, curly arms, which are used for feeding whilst the animal lies buried beneath the sand.

WILDFOWL

Two species of wildfowl are directly associated with seagrass, grazing on the leaves, which they are able to digest. Research has shown that in the British Isles, Brent Geese, *Branta bernicla*, get the majority of their energy from feeding on the eelgrass *Zostera marina*. These birds breed in the Arctic, with large numbers migrating south to overwinter in Britain. They can be seen rafting on the water waiting for the tide to drop low enough for them to reach the seagrass leaves. Disturbance at this time is a problem, as they are unable to reach deep enough at high tide. The Wigeon, *Anas penelope*, also relies on seagrass as a source of energy and its recent dramatic decline is believed to be partly linked to the decline of this food source.

A flock of Brent Geese feeding on seagrass at low tide.

A male Wigeon with its distinctive yellow forehead.

THE AUTHORS

Over the years we have carried out a variety of research projects around seahorses, their habitat and community. We have designed and built our own nocturnal light trap and baited remote underwater video system (BRUVS). The first was to sample small seahorse prey and discover if its arrival in abundance coincided with the spring arrival of seahorses on the site for breeding. The latter was designed to gather evidence that our local seagrass meadows in Dorset provide an important nursery ground for Undulate Rays. While the BRUVS failed to record the juvenile rays, it did record the astonishing abundance of juvenile fish and crustaceans that appear once the divers have retreated. Our records have been passed on to the relevant recording schemes and authorities to add weight to proposals for designation of Studland Bay as a Marine Protected Area.

Julie observes a pregnant male Spiny Seahorse during a dive.

Steve about to deploy his home-made nocturnal light trap in an effort to record the arrival of the seahorse's food.

The BRUVS in action.

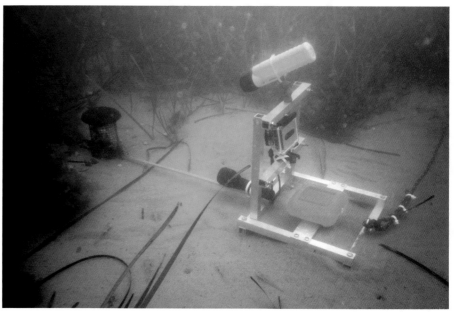

Undulate Ray research

While collecting mermaid's purses from beaches in Dorset as part of The Shark Trust's national survey, we noticed that a very high percentage of those picked up on both Studland and Swanage beaches were of the Undulate Ray. We had also seen very small Undulate Rays whilst diving there. Guessing that there was a spawning area for this endangered species nearby, and that the seagrass meadows in both bays were acting as a nursery area, we set about to prove this. We recruited volunteers to carry out dedicated eggcase surveys on Dorset beaches and divers to participate in underwater surveys. Our findings have been used in proposals to designate Studland Bay as a Marine Protected Area.

Julie surveying a sandy gully, on the look out for juvenile Undulate Rays.

A juvenile Undulate Ray measuring 15cm across the wingtips found in its seagrass meadow nursery.

Filming for TV

Going public with our frequent sightings of seahorses at Studland created an unexpected media frenzy. At the time, very few people knew that seahorses existed in the British Isles. We encouraged this TV coverage in an attempt to create public awareness that these rare and enigmatic animals were part of our native fauna. As a result we were in demand, working alongside TV production companies, including the BBC Natural History Unit, and were able to take some very enthusiastic presenters into the seagrass meadows to show them their first British seahorse. The understanding generated by these programmes has fuelled people's love of our native seahorses and their desire to see them protected, which was always our aim.

Cameramen filming seahorses underwater in the seagrass meadow

Steve being filmed kitting up prior to showing the film crew their first British seahorse.

Underwater filming

Back in 2008, as part of a campaign by marine conservation organisations in the UK, underwater film-maker Doug Anderson was commissioned to record some of the country's most iconic marine species, including the seahorses we had discovered in Studland Bay. We were tasked with finding seahorses for him and his team to film. This was very exciting for us, as Doug is one of the most highly regarded wildlife cameramen in the world, having worked on some of Sir David Attenborough's epic series including the BBC's Blue Planet, Frozen Planet and Life.

Working alongside Doug was a real eye-opener, and it was a privilege to watch, first-hand, the craft of underwater film-making. It is not just about jumping in the water for a few minutes and pointing a camera, but requires patience and understanding of the subject, sitting for hours at a time capturing subtle behaviour as the animal goes about its business. It is about composition of the shot, the way he positions himself to capture the bigger picture of the ecosystem, including shoals of bass swimming above while the seahorse carries on feeding, seemingly unconcerned, on the seabed below. The equipment is pretty impressive too! Our small underwater camera seemed insignificant next to the state-of-the-art kit Doug was wielding.

One of the majestic male Spiny Seahorses found on the shoot.

Underwater film-maker,
Doug Anderson, in his office.

REFERENCES

This book is based almost completely on our own experience and knowledge gained over many years but for some of the information we have sought guidance from the following sources. We would also recommend them as reference guides for further information.

Books

Cleave, A. & Sterry, P. 2012. *Collins Complete Guide to British Coastal Wildlife*. HarperCollins Publishers.

Hayward, P.J. & Ryland, J.S. 1995. *Handbook of the Marine Fauna of North-west Europe*. Oxford University Press.

Hayward, P., Nelson-Smith, T. & Shields, C. 1996. *Collins Pocket Guide – Seashore of Britain and Europe*. HarperCollins Publishers.

Henderson, P. 2014. *Identification Guide to the Inshore Fish of the British Isles*. Pisces Conservation Ltd.

Kay, P. & Dipper, F. 2009. *A Field Guide to the Marine Fishes of Wales and Adjacent Waters*. Marine Wildlife.

Naylor, P. 2011. *Great British Marine Animals (3rd Edition)*. Sound Diving Publications.

Trewhella, S. & Hatcher, J. 2015. *The Essential Guide to Beachcombing and the Strandline*. Wild Nature Press.

Papers

Lancaster, J. (Ed.), McCallum, S., Lowe A.C., Taylor, E., Chapman A. & Pomfret, J. (2014). *Development of detailed ecological guidance to support the application of the Scottish MPA selection guidelines in Scotland's seas*. Scottish Natural Heritage Commissioned Report No. 491. Eelgrass Beds – supplementary document.

Curtis, J.M.R. *Life History, Ecology and Conservation of European Seahorses*. (2004). McGill University, Montreal, Quebec, Canada.

Websites

Project Seahorse **www.projectseahorse.org**

Project Seagrass **www.projectseagrass.org**

UK Marine Special Areas of Conservation Project **www.ukmarinesac.org.uk/communities/zostera/z3_2.htm#a3**

iSeahorse **www.iseahorse.org**

The Marine Life Information Network **www.marlin.ac.uk**

Steve Trewhella Photography **www.ukcoastalwildlife.co.uk**

GLOSSARY

Asexual reproduction – a method by which a single parent can produce offspring. The offspring are genetically identical to the parent as there is no contribution of genetic material from a second parent.

Barbel – a finger-like sensory organ near the mouth of certain types of fish.

Bivalve – a mollusc with a pair of hinged shells

Byssus threads – strong, fine threads made of protein which are produced by some bivalve molluscs to attach themselves to hard substrates.

Carapace – the part of a crab shell that covers the head and body.

Cephalopod – a type of predatory marine mollusc, including octopus and squid, with a highly modified body. They have tentacles for catching prey and an ink sac for defence. In most the shell is internal or absent.

Chromatophore – a pigment-containing cell enabling an animal to change their colour. Most often used for camouflage.

Cnidaria (Cnidarians) – a large and very varied group of animals including sea anemones, jellyfish, hydroids and corals, which all have stinging capsules or nematocysts. They have two major stages in their life cycle: the medusa, free-swimming stage and the polyp, sessile (attached) stage.

Cryptic – camouflaged and therefore difficult to spot in its natural environment.

Detritivore – an animal which feeds on dead organic material.

Echinoderm – the name means 'spiny skin' and refers to a group of animals including starfish, sea urchins and sea cucumbers. Their body plan is based on five equal parts arranged around a central point.

Exoskeleton – the hard, protective outer layer found in some invertebrates such as crustaceans.

Fluoresce – to radiate light of a different wavelength to that absorbed, creating the appearance of glowing and colour change under certain light conditions.

Gastropod – a type of mollusc with a single, often coiled, shell as in snails, or an internal or absent shell as in slugs.

Mantle – the body wall of a mollusc which may be extended to form a siphon, for example in bivalves, or the foot in gastropods.

Periostracum – the flaky outer skin or coating on some bivalves.

Photosynthesis – the process used by plants and algae to trap the energy from sunlight, using carbon dioxide and water, and convert it into glucose. Oxygen is a by-product of this process.

Pliocene – an epoch in geological time roughly extending from 2.6 million years ago to 5.3 million years ago.

Ovipositor – a tube-like organ used by a female to implant her eggs in a cavity.

Radula – the toothed, ribbon-like structure used by gastropods to rasp and break off particles of vegetable matter for ingestion.

Rafting – A dense group of swimming seabirds or sea mammals.

Rhizome – a horizontal, underground stem of a plant from which new shoots can arise periodically along its length.

Rostrum – a projection, snout-like in shape, from the head of an animal.

Siphon – a long, tube-like structure; part of the anatomy of some molluscs.

Stranding – a marine plant, animal or object washed up on to the seashore above the waterline.

Symbiotic – a type of relationship between two species where both parties benefit.

Test – the outer shell or exoskeleton of a sea urchin.

Tube-feet – a system of multiple small projections that are moved by hydraulic pressure and used by echinoderms for locomotion, feeding and respiration.

ACKNOWLEDGEMENTS

As divers in British seas, we have been privileged to see at firsthand many wonderful marine creatures. The seahorse was never one that we expected to encounter. It was only on hearing about a local seahorse sighting by Dr Lin Baldock that these animals found their way on to our wish list. Her sighting and accompanying photographs inspired our desire to seek out our own seahorse, albeit only with a vague hope of succeeding. Lin has since become a good friend and, as a professional and hugely experienced ecologist has helped us, and others, to increase our understanding of these elusive animals.

We also owe a debt of gratitude to our friends Dr Ken Collins and Jenny Mallinson for their tireless efforts, producing peer-reviewed science in support of calls for the protection of seagrass meadows and seahorses, which are under threat in the British Isles and around the world.

This book would not be what it is without the support and expertise of a number of people to whom we owe our thanks. We have been extremely lucky to work, once again, with Julie Dando and Marc Dando at Wild Nature Press, whose experience and creative skills have transformed our vision for this book into a reality. Marc's illustrations add an extra dimension to our understanding of the wildlife and habitats described, capturing detail that photographs cannot show. We must also mention Rowena Millar for her editing expertise and knowledge. For kindly writing the foreword and for being an inspiration to divers and wildlife lovers everywhere through his stunning natural history film-making, we would like to thank Doug Allan.

Finally we would like to thank all those people who have dived with us, helped with surveys and allowed us to use their sightings, photographs and film, with the ultimate goal of making sure that wild seahorses are with us for a very long time to come. While we cannot name everyone, we would particularly like to single out Doug Anderson, Andy Jackson and Suzanne Munnelly.

Photographic credits

All photos are by Steve Trewhella and Julie Hatcher except those stated below. The authors and the publishers would like to thank those who have provided photographs.

Greg Balfour Evans/Alamy Stock Photo, page 8
Fred Bavendam/Minden Pictures/FLPA, page 11
blue-sea.cz/Shutterstock, page 12
Jure Žalohar, page 13 (from the Hitij & Žalohar Paleontological Collection, which is registered according to Slovenian legislation with the Natural History Museum of Slovenia)
Paul D Stewart/Nature Picture Library, page 26
Paul Parsons, page 32
Stephane Bidouze/Shutterstock, page 55
age fotostock/Alamy Stock Photo, page 98
Lin Baldock, pages 218 and 226 bottom left
Paul Naylor, pages 119, 121 and 207
Ernie Janes/Nature Picture Library, page 224

Spiny seahorse photographed by Lin Baldock in The Fleet Lagoon, Dorset – our inspiration!

INDEX

Photographic entries are in italic.